GUITAR
Identification

GUITAR Identification

4th edition

by A.R. Duchossoir

A Reference for Dating Guitars Made by Fender, Gibson, Gretsch, and Martin

HAL•LEONARD®
CORPORATION

7777 W. BLUEMOUND RD. P.O. BOX 13819 MILWAUKEE, WI 53213

ISBN 978-1-4234-2611-0

Published by:
Hal Leonard Corporation
7777 W. Bluemound Road
P.O. Box 13819
Milwaukee, WI 53213

Library of Congress Cataloging-in-Publication Data

Duchossoir, A. R.
  Guitar identification : a reference for dating guitars made by Fender,
Gibson, Gretsch, and Martin / by A. R. Duchossoir. -- 4th ed.
      p. cm.
  Includes bibliographical references (p.   ).
  ISBN 978-1-4234-2611-0
  1. Guitar--Identification. 2. Electric guitar--Identification. I. Title.
  ML1015.G9D9 2008
  787.87'19--dc22
                              2008019359

Printed in the U.S.A.

Fourth Edition

Visit Hal Leonard Online at **www.halleonard.com**

CONTENTS

PREFACE

Guitar Identification is a reference workbook meant for dating the American guitars made by Fender, Gibson, Gretsch, and Martin, thanks to the information derived from their serial numbers. As already mentioned in past editions, however, the following remarks should be borne in mind when consulting this book:

- Reliable records of serial numbers are not always available for all the makes and time periods covered in this book. The "meaning" of some numbers is based on actual factory ledgers while, for others, it is derived from a purely practical knowledge.

- Identification numbers are sometimes not sufficient to assess the vintage of certain instruments. This book also describes a few generic features typical of each brand, which can be of help for certain periods. In some cases, however, detailed information on a specific model and its historical whereabouts may prove indispensable for a more accurate dating.

- Nothing replaces first-hand experience, and the information supplied in this book should be actively supplemented by diligent homework at field level in order to gain a minimum of knowledge on each brand.

This updated edition of *Guitar Identification* is designed to include serial numbers up to early 2007 while fine-tuning or editing, where appropriate, the information contained in past editions.

Now that American manufacturers manage to convincingly duplicate their hallowed models from days gone by—including some of their typical vintage appointments—serial numbers may provide a useful key in distinguishing between older and newer guitars. Were it not for their specific serial numbers and conspicuous brand stamps, the relic'ed Fender Time Machine models or the Murphy-aged Les Paul Standard could be an embarrassing test for many! And with the ever-increasing prices of some vintage pieces, the "caveat emptor" rule should prevail.

A.R. Duchossoir

April 2007

ACKNOWLEDGMENTS

The author wishes to extend his thanks to the following individuals for their contribution to the making of this book (past and present editions).

Patrice AILLOT • Patrice BASTIEN • Klaus BLASQUIZ • Walter CARTER • Boris CITOVICS • Nick CLARKE • Cedric COULBAUT • James DEURLOO • Dany GIORGETTI • Gordon DOW • Yves FARGE • Gérard FERAUD • Scott GRANT • George GRUHN • Barry HYMAN • Bob KETZAR • Annica KREUTER • Sue LANDAU • David LEED • Perry MARGOULEFF - Jacques MAZZOLENI – Luc MELINE - Jean-François NOE • John PAGE • John PEDEN • Roger PINCOTT • Alan ROGAN • Peter SCHELL • Friedman SCHELL • Jay SCOTT • Dan SMITH • Richard SMITH • Stan SNYDER • Philippe TIBAL • James WERNER

The Fender Electric Instrument Co. was founded in 1946 by Clarence Leo Fender (1909–1991) in Fullerton, California. Leo Fender built lap steel guitars and amps before marketing his first electric "Spanish" guitar, the Esquire, in 1950. The Esquire and its siblings, the Broadcaster and the Telecaster, are widely regarded today as the first commercially successful solid-body electrics.

Other innovative designs like the Precision Bass, the Stratocaster, or the Jazz Bass subsequently contributed to turning Fender into a major contender in the field of electric guitars and basses. In late 1964, Leo Fender and his partner, Don Randall, sold their business to media giant CBS. Announced in January, 1965, the CBS takeover signalled a new era for Fender, albeit one gradually marked by quality problems and flagging creativity in establishing new models.

In January, 1985, 20 years after acquiring it, CBS disposed of Fender, and the company was purchased by a group of private investors led by Bill Schultz (1926–2006). Under the auspices of the new Fender Musical Instruments Corporation (F.M.I.C.), the production of U.S.-made guitars was relocated to a new plant in California while the corporate headquarters moved to Scottsdale, Arizona, during the 1990s. Today, the problems once caused by the CBS ownership are truly dead and gone, and the brand has reached new heights in popularity.

FOREWORD ON FENDER NUMBERS

Any lay reader should bear in mind that Fender serial numbers, at least up to 1976, were never meant to indicate, even vaguely, the date of issue of an instrument. They were intended strictly for registration purposes in relation to the original owner. Moreover, the way Fender electrics were built and assembled during the 1950s and 1960s strongly suggests that no articulate system was ever devised to allocate numbers in chronological fashion. Despite the empirical approach that may have prevailed, it is nonetheless possible to make some sense out of Fender numbers for dating purposes.

Various serialization schemes have been used since 1950, and their usefulness in this respect differs according to the styles and periods under consideration. Seemingly identical serial numbers may surface on different instruments of different vintage. For instance, symbolic numbers like 01, 001, 0001, L00001, 000001, V000001 all exist, sometimes in duplicates or triplicates on Fender guitars made at different periods.

Consequently, the first step in any research should be to log the correct serialization scheme in order to determine which dating mode may apply. This mode will usually take advantage of the fact that most Fender instruments feature date markings either on the neck, the body, or even the pickups. As a rule among guitar buffs and collectors, the neck date is widely considered the reference for a Fender because of its greater availability and/or visibility.

In late 1976 Fender switched to date-coded serial numbers purported to indicate the year of issue. This initiative was welcome because neck markings had ceased to reveal any explicit date since spring 1973. In the early 1980s the dating of the neck was reinstated with the vintage reissue models, thereby recreating a very useful Fender appointment. The neck date (if any) is indeed the surest way to date a Fender instrument.

The following paragraphs describe the various serialization schemes used by Fender on their U.S.-made instruments since 1950 and include comments on their usefulness for dating purposes. Models made in Japan, Korea, or Mexico are not within the purview of this book even though they often carry serial numbers that may confusingly duplicate American systems. These offshore instruments normally display a small decal on the headstock or on the back of the neck indicating the country of origin.

THE EARLY BESPOKE SERIES: 1950-1954

The earliest Fender electric guitars were not registered in a common serialization scheme, but each model or family was given its own four-digit series (Note: a zero counts as a digit).

Style and Location

The instruments produced between 1950 and 1954 can be regrouped in three "families":

1. The Esquire, Broadcaster, Telecaster, and what collectors refer to as the "No-Caster," i.e., a transition model between the Broadcaster and the Telecaster marketed in 1951 with no name except Fender on the peghead. All these models have four-digit numbers stamped on the bridge base plate, which, between 1950 and late 1954, run from 0001 to numbers in the 5000s.

2. The Precision Bass, first made in late 1951, also has a four-digit number stamped on its (smaller) bridge base plate. Its bespoke series runs from 0001 to the high 1000s between 1951 and early 1955.

3. The Stratocaster, marketed in spring 1954, also displays a four-digit number initially stamped on the vibrato back plate. These earliest numbers on the vibrato cover are in the 0100s and above. However, when the serial number was relocated to the neck plate in mid-1954, numbers lower than 0100 were also used. Overall the short-lived Stratocaster series runs from 0001 to the low 1000s, mostly through 1954.

Comments on Usefulness

Having three bespoke series of identical format means that a number like, say, 0166 can be found on three different models of different vintage, i.e., a 1950 Broadcaster, a 1952 Precision Bass, and a 1954 Stratocaster. Besides, within a given family, numbers do not necessarily progress in chronological order. For instance:

Early 1950s number (1126) stamped on the bridge plate of a "No-Caster"

1980s vintage number (10914) stamped on the bridge plate of a '52 Telecaster reissue. Note the dot stamped below the numerals to avoid possible confusion with a 1950s number.

#1106 belongs to a Telecaster with a January '54 neck date

#1292 belongs to an Esquire with a June '51 neck date

In short, the early bespoke series, on their own, are not particularly helpful in pinpointing the date of issue of a model—except, of course, 1954 Stratocasters. Whenever possible, it is recommended to check the date markings penciled at the heel of the neck under the truss rod adjusting bolt.

For further reference, table A shows a selection of early serial numbers and neck dates found on Telecaster-style instruments while table B presents a similar selection of early Precision Bass and Stratocaster numbers.

Serial number (0849) stamped on the bridge plate of a 1953 Precision Bass

R-number (R3999) on a Nocaster from the Time Machine series

1954 neck plate number

Late 1950s number with minus sign

Early 1960s number

1960s L-series number

1960s F-series number

1970s F-series number

Early Vintage Series number (V000049)

Time Machine neck plate number (R15055)

Custom Shop C-number from 1995 (CN507875)

Custom Shop C-number from 2005 (CZ502997) on a limited edition model

ESQUIRE/BROADCASTER/TELECASTER 1950–1954
Selected numbers with corresponding neck dates

No.	Date	Model	No.	Date	Model	No.	Date	Model
0017	11-50	Broadcaster	1688	2-51	Broadcaster	3566	7-52	Esquire
0052	12-50	Broadcaster	1734	2-51	Esquire	3747	10-52	Telecaster
0115	10-50	Broadcaster	1788	3-52	Esquire	3849	8-53	Telecaster
0210	7-51	Esquire	1895	9-51	Telecaster	3962	9-53	Esquire
0409	1-52	Esquire	1924	8-51	Nocaster	4046	1-53	Telecaster
0582	4-51	Nocaster	2023	10-53	Esquire	4124	2-53	Esquire
0591	11-50	Broadcaster	2112	8-52	Telecaster	4198	3-54	Telecaster
0690	2-51	Esquire	2190	7-53	Esquire	4204	8-52	Telecaster
0742	12-50	Broadcaster	2323	5-53	Telecaster	4303	3-52	Telecaster
0856	5-51	Esquire	2522	9-52	Telecaster	4551	4-53	Esquire
0936	9-51	Esquire	2782	4-54	Esquire	4676	8-54	Telecaster
1001	5-51	Nocaster	2961	12-53	Telecaster	4902	11-52	Telecaster
1072	9-51	Telecaster	3065	7-52	Telecaster	5032	10-53	Telecaster
1288	12-51	Telecaster	3158	9-53	Telecaster	5171	6-53	Telecaster
1396	11-51	Telecaster	3224	5-52	Telecaster	5204	7-52	Esquire
1427	8-51	Nocaster	3454	11-52	Esquire	5279	5-52	Telecaster
1587	12-52	Telecaster	3482	2-53	Esquire			

PRECISION BASS 1951–1955
Selected numbers with corresponding neck dates

No.	Date	No.	Date
0008	3-52	0730	5-54
0015	1-52	0788	12-54
0058	10-52	0856	4-53
0154	6-52	0975	7-53
0212	11-51	1139	3-55
0327	12-51	1275	11-54
0427	7-52	1301	3-53
0457	1-52	1394	6-54
0573	12-52	1409	3-55
0608	2-53	1897	9-54

STRATOCASTER 1954
Selected numbers with corresponding neck dates

No.	Date	No.	Date
0001	6-54	0694	10-54
0089	7-54	0705	8-54
0159	3-54	0810	11-54
0166	5-54	0835	9-54
0209	5-54	0948	8-54
0246	4-54	0985	11-54
0335	5-54	1052	10-54
0463	7-54	1063	11-54
0519	6-54	1108	9-54
0619	9-54	1122	12-54

THE ORIGINAL COMMON SERIES: 1954–1963

In 1954 it was resolved to discontinue the use of three bespoke series for each family of models and to issue all numbers from a single scheme.

Style and Location

The changeover was completed after late 1954, and by 1955 only one type of serial number was used. Regardless of the model, it was stamped on the upper edge of the neck plate as on the Stratocaster, while the Esquire and Telecaster rankings, then in the 5000s, served as the common basis. Interestingly, some Precision Basses from 1955 may feature two distinct numbers, one on the bridge plate (e.g., the old style #0753) and another one on the neck plate (e.g., the new style #8588).

No.	Date	Model	No.	Date	Model	No.	Date	Model	No.	Date	Model
5883	5-55	Esquire	20030	3-57	Esquire	43125	11-59	Stratocaster	72962	12-61	Stratocaster
6579	12-54	Stratocaster	20228	9-57	P. Bass	44157	6-60	Tele.Custom	73034	2-62	Bass VI
6608	3-55	Telecaster	21058	6-57	Stratocaster	44618	5-60	P. Bass	74611	MAR 62	Jazz Bass
6711	9-55	Esquire	21921	7-57	Duo Sonic	45301	1-60	Stratocaster	74708	3-62	Stratocaster
6777	11-54	Telecaster	22214	4-57	Musicmaster	45702	12-59	P. Bass	75940	1-62	Stratocaster
6805	1-55	Stratocaster	-22459	5-57	P. Bass	46136	2-60	P. Bass	76192	APR 62	Jazz Bass
6922	11-54	Esquire	022558)	12-57	Stratocaster	46773	5-60	Stratocaster	77303	JUL 62	Bass VI
7043	10-54	Esquire	-23811)			47045	3-60	Telecaster	77357	2-62	P. Bass
7145	1-55	P. Bass	022685)	1-58	Stratocaster	48983	6-60	Jazzmaster	78064	1-62	Jazzmaster
7336	8-54	Esquire	-23972)			49518	5-60	Telecaster	78426	OCT 62	Stratocaster
7512	6-55	P. Bass	022878)	2-59	Musicmaster	50032	5-60	Telecaster	78593	DEC 62	Duo Sonic
7774	1-56	Stratocaster	-23611)			50236	8-60	Jazz Bass	78689	SEP 62	Jaguar
8019	7-55	Telecaster	023072	3-59	Telecaster	51337	6-60	Duo Sonic	79124	JUN 62	Jazz Bass
8293	10-54	Telecaster	023078	1-58	P. Bass	51500	5-60	Stratocaster	79200	3-62	Stratocaster
8583	6-55	Stratocaster	-23685	11-57	Stratocaster	51593	12-59	P. Bass	80181	MAY 62	Jazzmaster
8588)	9-55	P. Bass	023864)	10-57	Esquire	52459	9-60	Duo Sonic	81587	JUN 63	Jaguar
0753)			-25085)			53171	8-60	Telecaster	81745	12-61	Esquire
08863	4-56	Stratocaster	024154)	12-57	Telecaster	54360	8-60	Esquire	82502	OCT 62	P. Bass
08948	5-55	Telecaster	-24785)					Custom	83323	AUG 62	Jazzmaster
08970	5-56	Esquire	024938	3-58	P. Bass	54983	10-60	Jazz Bass	83502	MAR 63	Telecaster
						55032	11-60	P. Bass			
09011	4-56	Stratocaster	025167	12-57	Esquire				83561	JUL 62	Jazz Bass
09145	4-56	P. Bass	025240	3-58	Stratocaster	55531	3-61	Stratocaster	84214	MAY 62	Bass VI
09542	11-55	Stratocaster	026315	7-58	Musicmaster	56090	2-61	Jazzmaster	85092	3-62	Jazzmaster
09563	2-56	P. Bass	026991	12-58	Stratocaster	56527	9-60	Jazz Bass	86042	AUG 62	P. Bass
09662	12-55	Telecaster	027110	3-58	P. Bass	57791	12-60	Jazzmaster	87551	MAY 62	Esquire Cust.
09890	3-56	Stratocaster	027699	5-58	Stratocaster	58020	10-60	Tele.Custom	87983	DEC 62	Stratocaster
10083	8-55	Telecaster	028343	4-58	Telecaster	58644	7-60	Musicmaster	88062	NOV 62	Jazz Bass
10546	11-55	Stratocaster	29039	8-58	P. Bass	59250	1-61	Jazzmaster	89227	JUL 62	Bass VI
10608	2-56	Telecaster	29587	9-58	Telecaster	59909	4-61	Esquire	89608	MAR 63	Stratocaster
11201	6-56	P. Bass	30108	10-58	Stratocaster	60138	2-61	Esquire	89686	JAN 63	Duo Sonic
						60625	12-59	Stratocaster			
11592	10-56	Musicmaster	30688	11-58	Stratocaster				89932	JUN 63	Bass VI
12319	7-56	Stratocaster	31418	1-59	Telecaster	61429	6-61	Stratocaster	90055	NOV 62	Jaguar
12842	8-55	Esquire	31454	12-58	P. Bass	61877	5-61	Jazz Bass	90080	DEC 62	Telecaster
13160	9-56	Stratocaster	31487	12-58	Jazzmaster	62213	4-61	Stratocaster	91264	DEC 63	Stratocaster
13676	12-56	Musicmaster	32577	10-58	Telecaster	62574	7-61	Jazzmaster	91877	MAY 62	Esquire
14093	8-56	Stratocaster	32699	7-59	Jazzmaster	63659	10-61	Musicmaster	91831	SEP 62	P. Bass
14897	1-57	P. Bass	33434	2-59	Telecaster	64061	6-61	Stratocaster	92255	DEC 62	Jazzmaster
15304	7-56	Telecaster	33838	1-59	Jazzmaster	64811	9-61	Jazzmaster	92430	APR 63	Stratocaster
15969	10-56	Stratocaster	34198	11-58	P. Bass	65507	8-61	Jazz Bass	93875	JUN 62	Esquire Cust.
16035	11-56	Esquire	34981	4-59	Telecaster	66168	6-61	Duo Sonic	94418	MAY 63	Stratocaster
						66673	10-61	Musicmaster			
16555	3-57	P. Bass	35013	2-59	Stratocaster				94797	FEB 63	Stratocaster
16720	8-57	Stratocaster	35337	3-59	Telecaster	67001	6-61	Telecaster	95436	AUG 62	Bass VI
16842	10-56	Duo Sonic	36251	3-59	Duo Sonic	67205	9-61	P. Bass	95782	MAY 63	Jaguar
17377	5-57	P. Bass	36278	12-58	Stratocaster	68183	11-61	Jazz Bass	96531	JAN 63	Musicmaster
17845	7-57	Musicmaster	37187	4-59	P. Bass	69687	8-61	Stratocaster	96846	DEC 62	Jazzmaster
18329	4-57	Stratocaster	38128	6-59	Musicmaster	69989	APR 62	Stratocaster	97339	MAY 63	Telecaster
18817	2-57	Telecaster	38188	11-58	Jazzmaster	70249	11-61	Jazz Bass	98440	APR 63	Duo Sonic
19211	1-57	P. Bass	39686	5-59	Jazzmaster	70282	10-61	Bass VI	99203	FEB 63	Jaguar
19459	2-57	Duo Sonic	39948	3-59	Jazzmaster	71059	12-61	Telecaster	99247	APR 63	Musicmaster
19886	5-57	Stratocaster	40644	10-58	Telecaster	71642	JUN 62	Stratocaster	99817	DEC 62	Esquire
						72711	10-61	Telecaster			

What is sometimes referred to as the original series ran from 1955 until 1963, with four- and then five-digit numbers roughly progressing in consecutive order from numbers in the 6000s up to 99,999. As Fender expanded its production, larger quantities of pre-stamped neck plates were ordered, and some of them show peculiar features that do not invalidate the overall dating guidelines.

For instance:

- Between 1955 and 1956 many plates were stamped with five-digit numbers beginning with 0 (e.g., 06998 or 09088) instead of straight four-digit numbers.
- Between 1957 and early 1958 many numbers in the 10,000s and 20,000s were stamped with a dash or minus sign ahead of the number (e.g., –17140 or –22770).
- Between late 1957 and late 1958 many plates were stamped with six-digit numbers beginning with 0 (e.g., 024077 or 028343) instead of straight five-digit numbers.
- Between late 1957 and late 1958 some plates were double-stamped and feature two different numbers on each side. As a rule, the visible number is of the six-digit type beginning with 0 (e.g., 024154), while the hidden number stamped on the underside is of the minus type (e.g., –24785).
- Between late 1959 and mid-1960 some numbers in the 40,000s and 50,000s were stamped on the *lower* edge of the neck plate instead of the upper edge.

Comments on Usefulness

The numbers used between 1955 and 1963 do not progress in perfect chronological order, but it is nevertheless possible to regroup them within a period of a year or so. For example, most of the numbers in the 30,000s are found on instruments with neck dates ranging from mid-1958 to late 1959. Of course, the neck date may precede the final assembly by a few weeks or months, but it is nonetheless a useful indication.

A few numbers, though, may not match the overall trend as their relevant neck plates may have been given the leftover treatment at the factory before being used on an instrument. Numbers off the main trend by two and even three years are known to exist—and may be plausible. A Fender neck plate may be easily swapped or replaced for whatever reasons! Whenever a more exact dating is required, it is again suggested to check out the actual neck date.

For further reference, table C shows a selection of instruments from the period 1954–1963 with their corresponding numbers and neck dates. The resulting pattern may be used to estimate the vintage of instruments with similar serial numbers.

THE "L" SERIES: 1963–1965

Style and Location

The "L" series is in all probability the result of a stamping mistake. When numbers in the 90,000s hit the assembly line, fresh neck plates came in, but for some reason, they did not turn out with numbers in the 100,000s. Instead they displayed five-digit numbers preceded by the letter L, hence the L-series designation. This apparent hiccup remained uncorrected in the mid-'60s, and L-numbers ran from L00001 up to L99999.

Comments on Usefulness

The earliest L-numbers—but not necessarily the lowest—appeared on guitars with late 1962 neck dates, and they overlapped with the last numbers from the original series. The bulk of the L-series is found, however, on instruments made between early 1963 and mid-1965. A few L-numbers can surface on later instruments dating from 1966, but these are usually exceptions.

L-numbers were assigned on a roughly consecutive basis but without any strict sequential order. In terms of volume, however, it is worth noting that the series was used up in less than three years, thereby allowing for meaningful groupings for dating purposes.

For further reference, table D shows a selection of L-numbered instruments with their corresponding neck dates.

"L-SERIES" 1963–1965
Selected numbers with corresponding neck dates

No.	Date	Model	No.	Date	Model	No.	Date	Model
L00352	APR 63	Musicmaster	L34135	FEB 64	Jaguar	L71717	OCT 65	Jazz Bass
L00435	JUN 62	Bass VI	L39957	AUG 64	Telecaster	L71919	MAY 63	Bass VI
L02776	APR 63	Telecaster	L42091	NOV 64	Mustang	L72906	NOV 64	Stratocaster
L06807	MAY 63	Jazz Bass				L74328	APR 65	Jazz Bass
L07501	JUL 63	Jazzmaster	L42226	SEP 64	P. Bass	L77677	JAN 65	Duo Sonic
L13140	SEP 63	Stratocaster	L43635	JUL 64	Jaguar	L78314	NOV 65	Electric XII
L14769	AUG 63	Jazz Bass	L46883	JUN 64	Jazzmaster	L80912	MAY 65	Stratocaster
L15823	JUN 63	Tele.Custom	L47211	OCT 64	Stratocaster	L81523	JUN 65	Bass VI
L18766	OCT 63	Stratocaster	L48968	SEP 64	Duo Sonic	L85911	APR 65	Jazzmaster
L20755	JAN 64	Jaguar	L50133	NOV 64	Stratocaster	L88924	AUG 65	Stratocaster
			L56333	DEC 64	Jaguar	L89142	MAY 65	Jaguar
L20800	NOV 63	Telecaster	L57868	JAN 65	P. Bass	L91893	JUL 65	Jazzmaster
L22956	DEC 63	Stratocaster	L59054	NOV 64	Mustang	L92205	AUG 65	Musicmaster
L23288	OCT 63	Esquire	L62281	JAN 64	Jazz Bass	L93728	JUN 65	Mustang
L25274	MAR 64	Jazz Bass				L98675	SEP 65	Stratocaster
L29503	JUL 64	Stratocaster	L64537	JAN 65	Stratocaster	L98917	NOV 65	P. Bass
L31747	APR 64	Stratocaster	L65143	MAR 65	Jaguar	L99865	JUL 65	Stratocaster
L32062	JUN 64	Jazzmaster	L69910	FEB 65	Mustang			

THE "F" SERIES: 1965–1976

Style and Location

When L-numbers in the 90,000s came in sight on the production line around spring 1965, neck plates with six-digit numbers in the 100,000s were brought in, albeit without any L-prefix. The new plates were instead characterized by a big "F" conspicuously stamped below the number—hence the F-series designation. In the eyes of many collectors, these F-plates signal instruments from the CBS era, whereas those with L-plates are considered to be the last specimens from the Leo Fender era.

Because of drastically increased production after the mid-'60s, F-numbers moved up rapidly from 100,000s to the mid-700,000s in about 11 years. As was the case with the previous series, numbers were assigned in a roughly consecutive pattern without any strict chronological order between numbers.

Comments on Usefulness

The F-series is moderately useful for dating an instrument. A quick reading of a given number can at best allow for a dating within a year, and at worst within three years. If a more precise assessment is required, it is recommended to check out the neck date, often explicitly stated until spring 1973 (on instruments with numbers usually in the low 400,000s) and in coded form thereafter. Interestingly, as explained in this chapter, six-digit F-numbers may prove a more reliable guide than neck dates on certain models like the Custom/Maverick or the Swinger/Musiclander.

For further reference, table E shows a selection of instruments from the period 1965–1973 with their numbers and corresponding neck dates. For the F-numbers issued between 1973 and 1976, Fender ussued the following loose guidelines during the 1980s:

- 400,000s numbers: April 1973 to September 1976
- 500,000s numbers: September 1973 to September 1976
- 600,000s numbers: August 1974 to August 1976
- 700,000s numbers: September 1976 to December 1976

"F-SERIES" 1965–1973
Selected numbers with corresponding neck dates

No.	Date	Model	No.	Date	Model	No.	Date	Model	No.	Date	Model
100339	OCT 65	P. Bass	184295	AUG 66	Mustang	257730	MAY 69	Maverick	340706	JAN 72	Musicmaster B.
101017	SEP 65	Duo Sonic	185035	MAY 67	Bass VI	259809	SEP 69	Stratocaster	343637	DEC 71	Telecaster
103974	JUN 65	Jazzmaster	185970	MAY 66	P. Bass	261105	OCT 69	Jazz Bass	343870	MAY 72	P. Bass
104906	MAY 65	Telecaster	188665	SEP 66	Stratocaster	263118	MAY 69	Mustang Bass	344132	NOV 71	Bronco
105554	NOV 65	Mustang	190151	OCT 66	Jazzmaster	264593	MAY 66	Swinger	345558	APR 72	P. Bass
105974	JUN 65	Stratocaster	193381	DEC 66	Jaguar	265103	AUG 69	Telecaster	346073	FEB 72	Musicmaster B.
106787	NOV 65	P. Bass	193463	AUG 66	Esquire	265248	JAN 67	Swinger	349379	DEC 72	Telecaster
108498	NOV 65	Electric XII	194134	MAY 66	Electric XII	266642	NOV 67	Mustang Bass	349593	FEB 72	Jazz Bass
109165	AUG 65	Jazz Bass	194137	NOV 66	Stratocaster	268142	OCT 66	Jazzmaster	352189	APR 72	Tele. Bass
110668	OCT 65	Electric XII	197141	AUG 67	Telecaster	270535	MAY 69	P. Bass	352977	OCT 72	Tele. Bass
111274	DEC 65	Mustang	198954	MAY 67	Mustang Bass	271154	SEP 66	Swinger	354521	SEP 72	Stratocaster
112172	SEP 66	Telecaster	199929	JUN 67	Telecaster	272502	MAR 71	Tele. Thinline	355538	MAR 72	Stratocaster
113399	NOV 65	Jazz Bass	200265	SEP 66	Coronado	275152	SEP 69	Telecaster	356969	FEB 72	Tele. Custom
115151	FEB 66	Esquire	201428	JUN 67	Telecaster	278916	MAY 70	Tele. Bass	357231	OCT 71	Tele. Thinline
117648	APR 66	Electric XII	202740	MAY 66	Mustang	278927	MAR 71	Stratocaster	358541	JUN 72	Jazzmaster
199049	JAN 66	Jazzmaster	204632	SEP 67	Stratocaster	280816	AUG 70	Tele. Thinline	359413	FEB 73	P. Bass
120435	NOV 65	Jazz Bass	205084	DEC 67	Jazz Bass	283092	JAN 68	Stratocaster	361531	AUG 72	Telecaster
121880	FEB 66	Stratocaster	206900	FEB 67	P. Bass	283782	NOV 69	Jazz Bass	363204	SEP 72	P. Bass
123868	DEC 65	Jaguar	207186	DEC 66	Mustang	286193	JUL 68	Tele. Thinline	364766	APR 72	Jazz Bass
125772	SEP 65	Stratocaster	208410	SEP 67	Esquire Cust.	290835	JUL 69	Mustang	365444	JUN 72	P. Bass
127437	MAY 66	P. Bass	209748	NOV 67	Bronco	292960	OCT 70	Tele. Thinline	367487	APR 72	Musicmaster
129377	APR 66	Electric XII	210524	OCT 67	Telecaster	293780	SEP 70	P. Bass	368074	JUL 72	Stratocaster
130787	FEB 66	Duo Sonic	211478	AUG 68	Tele. Bass	295668	NOV 71	Jazz Bass	369154	DEC 72	Tele. Bass
132860	MAR 66	Mustang	212517	DEC 67	Telecaster	297863	NOV 70	Telecaster	370311	APR 72	P. Bass
136892	MAY 66	Electric XII	214068	MAR 68	Mustang	299207	FEB 71	Stratocaster	370664	FEB 73	Jazz Bass
138070	FEB 66	Stratocaster	215697	OCT 66	P. Bass	300612	MAR 70	Tele. Thinline	371447	JUN 72	Telecaster
139039	JAN 66	Jazz Bass	216429	MAY 67	Bass VI	301369	JUN 72	P. Bass	373029	SEP 72	P. Bass
139227	DEC 65	Stratocaster	216977	DEC 67	Esquire	301463	JAN 71	Stratocaster	373353	OCT 72	Stratocaster
140431	APR 66	Jaguar	217144	NOV 67	Coronado	301922	OCT 70	Mustang	375511	AUG 72	Jazz Bass
142386	MAY 66	Duo Sonic	217379	FEB 68	Telecaster	303319	SEP 71	Mustang Bass	376380	FEB 73	Bronco
146013	JUN 66	Electric XII	220667	MAY 68	Telecaster P.	305413	DEC 70	Telecaster	377086	JAN 73	P. Bass
147397	OCT 65	P. Bass	220754	DEC 67	Jaguar	306690	APR 71	Stratocaster	378677	DEC 72	Jazz Bass
147622	MAR 66	P. Bass	221161	NOV 68	Tele. Bass	309040	OCT 71	Jazz Bass	380023	NOV 71	Stratocaster
147824	MAY 66	Tele. Custom	223504	SEP 68	Stratocaster	309373	JUL 71	Musicmaster	382821	MAR 72	Tele. Custom
149902	JUL 66	Mustang	224160	MAY 69	Jazz Bass	310967	APR 72	Telecaster	385422	FEB 73	Mustang
150627	APR 66	Jaguar	226131	AUG 66	Custom	313652	MAY 71	Musicmaster	387485	JAN 73	Jazz Bass
151206	JUN 66	Jazz Bass	228262	AUG 68	Mustang Bass	314139	NOV 72	Stratocaster	390437	AUG 72	Stratocaster
152826	MAR 67	Coronado	230599	FEB 67	Jazzmaster	315451	JAN 72	P. Bass	392328	OCT 72	Telecaster
154344	JAN 66	Electric XII	231520	DEC 68	Tele. Thinline	316015	DEC 72	Telecaster	393691	FEB 73	P. Bass
158432	JUN 66	Musicmaster	235157	AUG 68	Tele. Bass	316731	MAY 71	Musicmaster B.	395988	SEP 72	Telecaster
159174	APR 66	Telecaster	236163	SEP 68	Jazz Bass	316987	JAN 73	Telecaster	396176	JAN 73	Stratocaster
160552	MAY 66	P. Bass	237973	OCT 68	Stratocaster	317575	APR 71	Tele. Thinline	400055	MAR 73	Stratocaster
161736	APR 66	Stratocaster	238946	FEB 69	Telecaster	319891	NOV 70	Tele. Bass	400618	DEC 72	Tele. Thinline
162164	FEB 67	Coronado	239984	JUN 69	Tele. Bass	321153	AUG 71	P. Bass	404831	JUN 72	Jaguar
164209	JUN 66	Jazzmaster	240238	AUG 68	Telecaster	323057	MAY 71	Stratocaster	407156	FEB 73	Telecaster
167924	OCT 66	Telecaster	242245	APR 68	Stratocaster	325034	JAN 72	Telecaster	412357	APR 72	Telecaster
169551	AUG 66	Electric XII	244998	JUL 66	Custom	325108	NOV 71	Bronco	418357	MAR 73	Stratocaster
170416	MAR 66	Telecaster	247846	FEB 68	Jazz Bass	327902	AUG 71	Jazzmaster	419454	MAR 73	Tele. Thinline
171062	SEP 66	Jaguar	248571	MAR 68	Mustang Bass	328341	NOV 71	Jazz Bass	500641	JAN 66	Coronado
172229	OCT 66	Esquire	249563	JAN 68	Jazz Bass	330507	FEB 72	Telecaster	502230	JAN 67	Coronado
174713	AUG 66	Jaguar	250568	OCT 68	Tele. Bass	330646	SEP 71	Tele. Bass	502314	MAR 68	Coronado XII
176469	DEC 66	Jazz Bass	251663	APR 68	Stratocaster	334734	AUG 71	Mustang	600182	JAN 66	Bass V
179031	SEP 66	Mustang	253038	JUL 69	Jazz Bass	338002	SEP 71	Stratocaster	600959	OCT 67	Bass V
181317	NOV 66	Mustang Bass	255500	JAN 69	Tele. Custom	338182	FEB 73	Telecaster	602548	FEB 67	Bass V
182642	FEB 67	Coronado XII	255643	JUL 69	Stratocaster	338795	FEB 72	Telecaster	627740	JAN 68	Coronado

As a summary, table F provides a quick dating chart for the instruments made between 1954 and 1976 that have the serial number stamped on the neck plate (i.e., original series, L-Series, and F-series).

Bear in mind that some models may have numbers that do not fall within the basic pattern of F-numbers. For instance:

- American-made flat-top acoustics from the 1960s such as the Kingman, Malibu, or Villager feature bespoke four- and then five-digit numbers stamped on a blazon-like neck plate.
- The Coronado thinlines marketed in the second half of the 1960s may be found with numbers in the 500,000s and 600,000s, as well as with regular numbers in the 100,000s and 200,000s. The same holds true for the Bass V available between 1965 and 1970.
- The LTD and Montego, Fender's short-lived top-end archtop electrics, were issued between 1969 and 1975 with a specific two-digit number.

HEADSTOCK NUMBERS: 1976–PRESENT

In late 1976 the serial number ceased to be stamped on the neck plate and was moved onto the headstock decal next to the model designation. Fender also adopted a completely new date-coded serialization scheme.

Style and Location

The new-style seven-digit serial numbers applied on the front face of the peghead via a transfer first appeared in late 1976. They were designed to feature a two-digit prefix indicating the year of issue, complemented by five digits for the identification of the instrument on a roughly cumulative basis.

The earliest prefix used (briefly) by Fender was 76, clearly marked in bolder numerals, and serial numbers read 76xxxxx. This prefix was quickly discarded in favor of S6, where S simply stood for seventies. This modification heralded the advent of a system—tentatively called the decade system—that is still in use today on most of the Fender instruments made in the United States. In this system:

- The first digit in the prefix is a letter corresponding to the decade, i.e.:
  S = Seventies (1970s) • E = Eighties (1980s) • N = Nineties (1990s) • Z = Noughties (2000s)
- The second digit shows the year in the decade, hence a DYxxxxx(x) format.

For instance:

#S723115	=	1977 (S7)
#E900013	=	1989 (E9)
#N8346433	=	1998 (N8)
#Z3025922	=	2003 (Z3)
#Z7223251	=	2007 (Z7)

In the early 1990s the number of digits used for the identification of each instrument was increased from five to six to match the enlarged production.

As a quick rule of thumb, the number is applied on the front face of the headstock on instruments fitted with the modern Fender corporate logo. On models displaying the old-style "spaghetti" logo, the serial number is usually found on the back of the headstock.

The rationale behind the decade system (i.e., a DY prefix) has been subsequently applied, albeit inconsistently, to the Signature models (SDYxxxx) and to the Custom Shop models (CDYxxxxx). The American Deluxe series also uses it with an additional "real" D prefix (e.g., DZ6035799 for a 2006 instrument). It is also found on Fender offshore instruments made in Mexico, Japan, and Korea. For example, the Mexican-made instruments display an MDYxxxxx number whereas the California series models of joint origin carry an AMXDYxxxxx number with an ad hoc prefix.

Comments on Usefulness

The scheme pioneered in 1976 looks perfectly all right in principle, but it is not entirely reliable to date the instruments made by Fender in the U.S.A. Several factors explain this situation.

- At the end of each year, new decals reflecting the change in the year/prefix are ordered from a subcontractor, but the old ones are not instantly discarded at the beginning of each new year. Often the previous year's decals are used in a new year even though they no longer have the correct annual prefix. For instance, many 1980 and 1981 guitars were actually released with S9 numbers (1979).

- After CBS decided to dispose of Fender in mid-1984, no E5 decals were ordered. Until the Fullerton plant shut down in 1985, instruments were shipped with E4 (1984) and even E3 (1983) decals.

- When the newly-independent Fender company resumed production in the U.S.A. in 1985, it had a sizeable inventory of E4 decals to use up. Given the initially limited output of the new Corona plant, it took until 1988 to absorb all the leftover E4 decals. In other words, E5, E6, and E7 decals were never applied to U.S.-made instruments, but they do exist on Japanese-made Fender guitars. Moreover, some instruments meant for export to Europe were sometimes prefixed with EE.

- Because of what was presumably a mistake by the supplier, the first batch of 1990 decals came out with N9 (1999) instead of an N0 prefix. Those N9 decals were not, however, thrown away, and they surfaced on instruments made in 1990 and 1991, (e.g., on the Set Neck Telecasters made by the Custom Shop).

For a quick reference, the two-digit prefixes used since 1976 by Fender on its standard U.S. models are grouped in table G. Although the decade system remains today the main scheme found on Fender guitars, many new models or series have been assigned distinct serial numbers over the past 20 years as detailed on the next page.

1976 number with 76 prefix

1978 number with S8 prefix

1989 number with E9 prefix

Appearances may be deceptive. Despite its N9 prefix, this number belongs to a 1990 instrument. Because of a mistake in procurement, the earliest 1990 decals were numbered with N9 instead of N0.

1988 Signature number with SE8 prefix

1998 number with N8 prefix

COLLECTOR'S SERIES: 1981–1983

Style and Location

Briefly available in the early 1980s, the various models in the Collector's series were fitted with specific serial numbers featuring a bespoke two-digit prefix beginning with C for each model, i.e.:

CA for the Gold Stratocaster

CB for the Gold Jazz Bass

CC for the Walnut Strat

CD for the Walnut Precision Bass

CE for the Black and Gold Telecaster

The Gold Strat introduced shortly thereafter also featured CA in its number before shifting to a specific GO prefix, which was also used on the Gold Precision Special of the same period.

Comments on Usefulness

These Collector's numbers are not date-coded, and consequently their dating can only be approximate, even though their period of issue was relatively narrow. Fortunately, Fender began reinstating the dating of necks at about the same time they were issued!

Custom Shop number (CN201893) applied with a decal—but this does not belong to a 1992 instrument!

2006 number (DZ6102501) on a model from the Deluxe series

Typical number (X of Y) on a model from a Custom Shop limited run

Early four-digit Custom Shop number (0077) applied on the back of the headstock

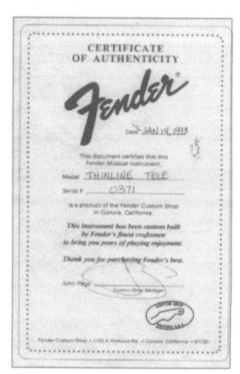

Certificate of Authenticity from the Custom Shop dated 14 January, 1993

TABLE F

NECK PLATE NUMBERS SUMMARY 1954–1976

Year	Typical Series
1954	four or five digits (beginning with 0) under 10,000
1955	four or five digits (beginning with 0) under 10,000; a few five digits in the low to mid-10,000s
1956	a few four or five digits (beginning with 0) under 10,000; five digits in the low to mid-10,000s
1957	five digits in the mid to high 10,000s; five digits in the low 20,000s
1958	five or six digits (beginning with 0) in the 20,000s; five digits in the low 30,000s
1959	five digits in the 30,000s; five digits in the low 40,000s
1960	five digits in the 40,000s and 50,000s
1961	five digits in the 50,000s and 60,000s; five digits in the low 70,000s
1962	five digits in the 60,000s, 70,000s, and 80,000s; five digits in the low 90,000s
1963	five digits in the 80,000s and 90,000s L+ five digits under 10,000 L+ five digits in the 10,000s and 20,000s
1964	L+ five digits in the 20,000s, 30,000s, 40,000s, and 50,000s
1965	L+ five digits in the 50,000s, 60,000s, 70,000s, 80,000s, and 90,000s; six digits in the low 100,000s
1966	six digits in the 100,000s and low 200,000s
1967	six digits in the high 100,000s and low 200,000s
1968	six digits in the mid-200,000s
1969	6 digits in the mid to high 200,000s; a few 6 digits in the low 300,000s
1970	6 digits in the high 200,000s and low 300,000s
1971	6 digits in the low to mid 300,000s
1972	6 digits in the 300,000s
1973	6 digits in the high 300,000s, 400,000s, and low 500,000s
1974	6 digits in the 400,000s, 500,000s, and low 600,000s
1975	6 digits in the high 400,000s, 500,000s, and 600,000s
1976	6 digits in the high 500,000s, 600,000s, and low 700,000s start of headstock numbers

TABLE G

DECADE PREFIX NUMBERS SUMMARY 1976–1999

Prefix	Typical Year
76	1976
S6	1976
S7	1977 with overlap in 1978
S8	1978 with overlaps in 1977 and 1979
S9	1979 with overlaps in 1980 and 1981
E0	1980 with overlaps in 1979 and 1981
E1	1981 with overlaps in 1980 and 1982
E2	1982 with overlaps in 1981 and 1983
E3	1983 with overlaps in 1982, 1984, and 1985
E4	1984 with overlaps in 1985, 1986, 1987, and 1988
E8	1988 with overlap in 1989
E9	1989 with overlap in 1990
N0	1990 with overlap in 1991
N1	1991 with overlap in 1992
N2	1992 with overlap in 1993
N3	1993 with overlap in 1994
N4	1994 with overlap in 1995
N5	1995 with overlap in 1996
N6	1996 with overlap in 1997
N7	1997 with overlap in 1998
N8	1998 with overlap in 1999
N9	1990 (by mistake) 1999 with overlap in 2000
Z0	2000 with overlap in 2001
Z1	2001 with overlap in 2002
Z2	2002 with overlap in 2003
Z3	2003 with overlap in 2004
Z4	2004 with overlap in 2005
Z5	2005 with overlap in 2006
Z6	2006 with overlap in 2007
Z7	2007 with overlap in 2008
Z8	2008 with potential overlap in 2009

THE VINTAGE SERIES: 1982–PRESENT

In late 1981 Fender announced the introduction of modern renditions of some of its most enduring classic designs: the '52 Telecaster, the '57 and '62 Stratocaster, the '57 and '62 Precision Bass, and the '62 Jazz Bass. These models have since become the cornerstones of Fender's electric guitar range.

Style and Location

With the exception of the '52 Telecaster, the American Vintage series models feature seven-digit serial numbers stamped on the neck plate. The numbers consist of a V prefix followed by six digits (i.e., a Vxxxxxx format). The '52 Telecaster reissue at first displayed a straight four-digit number (no V) stamped on the bridge base plate, before moving to a five-digit number (still no V) in the late 1980s.

Comments on Usefulness

The numbers in the Vintage series are not date-coded, and therefore, they are not very helpful on their own for dating an instrument. This situation is compounded by the duplication that took place between the CBS-era instruments made in Fullerton up to 1984 and the post-CBS ones made in Corona. When the new F.M.I.C. resumed the production of the vintage models in late 1985, the serialization scheme went back to #V000001! Therefore duplications in low V-numbers took place during the 1980s.

It should also be mentioned that many of the early Custom Shop limited production models, whether vintage reissues or not, were fitted with V-style neck plates picked up pretty much at random. As of 2007, neck plates with numbers above V165000 have become the norm on models from the Vintage series.

CUSTOM SHOP GUITARS: 1987–PRESENT

In 1987 Fender opened a separate Custom Design and Manufacturing facility to build one-off superlative guitars for artists and for trade shows. The success of the Custom Shop rapidly exceeded all expectations, and its product line has been constantly enlarged to encompass special renditions of classic Fender models (i.e., the Custom Classics), namesake models (i.e., Signature models), various limited and special editions, and since 1999, the production of the replicas from the Time Machine series.

Style and Location

The instruments produced by the Custom Shop can be found with many different types of serial numbers.

- The early one-off instruments built by the Shop's master luthiers (but not yet called "Masterbuilt") carry a four-digit number applied via a black decal on the back of the headstock. These numbers, sometimes also stamped on the neck plate, were meant to be consecutive and not date-coded.

- The more recent "Masterbuilt" models (as opposed to the notion of "team-built" models) can be found with a five-digit number consisting of the initials of the master luthier followed by a three-digit (so far) ranking number. For instance:

  #CF479 on a Chris Fleming instrument

  #JC520 on a John Cruz instrument

However, this system is not systematically used by all the master luthiers on all of their instruments.

- The early "customized" (read team-built) production models were fitted either with neck plates borrowed from the Vintage series (with a Vxxxxxx format) or with old decals from the CBS era (e.g., numbers from Collector's series), sometimes slightly modified to conceal their origin!

For instance:

V066617 on a Classic Player 1960 Stratocaster with a 9/23/93 certificate of authenticity

- As of 1991 the Custom Shop began implementing its own numbering scheme, which simply adds a C prefix to the decade system found on regular production models, thereby resulting in a CDYxxxx format, later enlarged to CDYxxxxx and to CDYxxxxxx.

For instance:

#CN30323	=	1993 (N3)
#CN700569	=	1997 (N7)
#CZ5000888	=	2005 (Z5)

These C-numbers are usually stamped on the neck plate, but they can also be applied with a decal on the headstock, for instance, on the Set Neck models.

Although they are designed to be date-coded, caution should be exercised with these numbers because they do not always indicate the exact year of issue of an instrument, at least in relation to the date featured on the certificate of authenticity that usually accompanies a Custom Shop instrument since 1989. For instance:

#CN201109 on a Telecaster Jr. with a COA dated October, 1995

#CN700268 on a WR Telecaster with a COA dated February, 1999

More recently, a limited run of '60 Stratocasters with racing stripes was fitted with a neck plate stamped with a CZ5xxxxx number (2005) and a bespoke mention "Limited Edition NAMM 2007."

- In early 1995 the Custom Shop began offering the Relic series, i.e., vintage models artificially aged to reproduce the look and feel of "used" classics from the '50s and '60s. The Relic models inaugurated a new numbering scheme consisting of four or five digits prefixed by the letter R, but without any direct reference to the year of issue.

Regardless of their type (Telecaster, Stratocaster, or Bass), all the Relic instruments issued until May, 1999, carry an Rxxxx number stamped on the neck plate. These instruments were actually painted, aged, and assembled externally by Vince Cunetto on behalf of the Custom Shop.

Beginning in late 1998, the production of the Relic models, supplemented by the Closet Classic and the New Old Stock (N.O.S.) variants, was gradually shifted back to the Custom Shop and relaunched under the Time Machine moniker. The series was also subsequently enlarged to incorporate many vintage models from the '50s to the '70s.

Thanks to a major retooling, the Time Machine instruments are far more historically accurate in their construction and details than the early Relics (which, however, may be prettier!) and the Vintage series. They basically come up with two variants of the R-number:

R+4 digits stamped on the bridge plate of mostly '50s style Telecasters with a maple neck, e.g., R4415. But Rxxxx numbers are also found on the early '63 style reissues.

R+5 digits stamped on the neck plate for all the '60s style instruments (including replicas of 1959 models with a rosewood fingerboard). For instance, R1xxxx, R2xxxx, or R3xxxx.

Rxxxxx numbers are also found on some signature (e.g., Robin Trower) and tribute models (e.g., Rory Gallagher).

- Recent additions to the Custom Shop production like the Stratocaster Pro and the Telecaster Pro have a four-digit number (e.g., 2741) with a 9 May 2006 neck date stamped on their contoured neck plate.

Comments on Usefulness

With the cautious exception of the date-coded CDYxxxx(xx) numbers, the Custom Shop models are not user-friendly for dating purposes. Fortunately, all the instruments produced by the Fender "Dream Factory" usually come with a certificate of authenticity indicating the date (or at the very least, the month) of issue.

Additionally, they normally feature a date marking on the neck, not accessible on the models with a set neck! They also display Custom Shop logos or Relic markings stamped into the wooden parts to avoid any confusion and potential attempts at forgery.

THE SIGNATURE MODELS: 1988–PRESENT

The so-called Signature (or namesake) models may be full production instruments made at the main Fender plant, built solely by the Custom Shop, or issued as a limited edition model. This explains why they can be found with different types of serial numbers, not always useful for dating purposes. The main numbering schemes used on them are as follows:

- Signature models like those endorsed by Jeff Beck, Roscoe Beck, Eric Clapton, Buddy Guy, Stu Hamm, Richie Sambora, and Stevie Ray Vaughan normally follow the same rationale as the standard decade system presented in the Headstock Numbers section (page 9). They just feature an additional S for Signature ahead of the two-digit prefix indicating the basic year of issue; hence, a basic SDYxxxxx format. For instance:

S.R. Vaughan Stratocaster	#SE910479	=	1989 (SE9)
Roscoe Beck Bass V	#SN6937030	=	1996 (SN6)
Jeff Beck Stratocaster	#SZ6000783	=	2006 (SZ6)

However, the date implied by the number cannot always be trusted at face value as, for example, a Stevie Ray Vaughan Stratocaster with number SE909569 (1989) comes with a 13 May, 1992, neck date. In fact, it often looks as if Fender is recycling outdated decals and neck plates on certain signature models. Thus SRV models often come with an SE9xxxxx number.

Likewise, the recent Mark Knopfler Stratocasters or the John Meyer Stratocasters made in the 2000s carry SE0xxxx numbers (1980) that show no relevance whatsoever to their actual date of issue. In such cases, the neck date is obviously the surest way to date the instrument.

- Other Signature models like the James Burton Telecaster or the Bonnie Raitt Stratocaster may display a regular production number reading DYxxxxxx. For instance:

James Burton Telecaster	#E802618	=	1988 (E8)
Bonnie Raitt Stratocaster	#N562422	=	1995 (N5)

However, Burton Telecasters are often found with numbers that show absolutely no relevance with the decade system, e.g., C900765 on a 2003 instrument. The latest variants of the model featuring flames instead of the paisley pattern are fitted with N4xxxxxx numbers (1994). Again, Fender appears to be recycling old numbers and decals on newer models. In such cases, the neck date is obviously the surest way to date the instrument.

- Conversely, Custom Shop instruments that are not signature models can sometimes be found with an SDYxxxxx style number that is being usefully recycled!

- The short-lived Jimi Hendrix Tribute Stratocaster displays a slightly different decade number, prefixed with a T and reading TDYxxxxx.

- Several of the Signature models built in relatively small quantities by the Custom Shop display bespoke numbers using the two initials of the artist as a prefix with three or four digits indicating a cumulative ranking. For instance:

    Clarence White Telecaster with #CW021

    Jerry Donahue Telecaster with #JD0925

A similar approach was retained for the limited edition Mary Kaye Stratocaster produced by the Custom Shop in 2005/2006, which displays numbers like MK5056 and MK5161.

The full production Eric Johnson Stratocaster introduced in 2005 has a similar number, prefixed by the initials of the artist, e.g., #EJ05158 and #EJ11435. The numbers prefixed with initials are not date-coded, and their vintage has to be achieved with the neck markings or the accompanying certificate (if any).

- Finally, as mentioned on page 14 regarding Time Machine instruments, some signature and tribute models are fitted with standard Rxxxxx numbers when they are based on a vintage model.

THE LIMITED EDITIONS: 1988–PRESENT

The earliest limited edition (LE) marketed as such by Fender was the 25th Anniversary Stratocaster from 1979, even though its production in the thousands hardly warrants a "limited" designation. As in the automotive industry, LEs of various sizes and shapes have now become a standard marketing ploy since the 1980s.

Style and Location

- The 25th Anniversary Stratocaster came out with a six-digit number beginning with "25" stamped on the neck plate at a time when numbers applied with a decal on the headstock were the norm. However, this number was not date-coded, and one has to refer to the accompanying certificate of merit to date the model. For example: #250025 with a certificate dated July 25, 1979.

- A fairly common style for numbering LE models took shape with the early Custom Shop runs where instruments were itemized via a ranking against total production (e.g., 098 of 100). Again, a certificate of authenticity is key to log the year of issue.

- Many recent LE models display a regular decade-style number but have a bespoke neck plate clearly indicating the LE status and the year of issue. For instance: "Limited Edition January NAMM 2005" with number CZ52267 on a '58-style Precision bass reissue.

- LE models like the masterbuilt 1954 Stratocaster made by the Custom Shop in 2004 have a four-digit number on the vibrato back plate that varies according to the master builder that made them. For instance, 5458 (with a smaller last digit) on a John Cruz, 4330 (smaller last digit, too) on a Mark Kendrick, or 5343 (no small digit) on a Yuriy Shishkov.

Comments on Usefulness

On their own, LE numbers are often useless to date an instrument. As is the case with instruments carrying a number that is not date-coded, the vintage can be assessed thanks to the neck markings. However, many LE models come with a certificate that normally shows the date of issue. Anniversary models are also easy to log even though their production may sometimes span more than a single year.

HELPFUL DATING FEATURES

Certain features, typical of Fender guitars, may help in assessing the vintage of a given instrument. They can contribute to substantiating the dating that may be derived from the serial number alone. This section looks at generic features likely to supplement the information suggested by serial numbers.

One particular problem with Fender instruments is that their method of construction can make them easier to modify than the guitars from Gibson, Gretsch, or Martin. Moreover the spectacular progress made by Fender (and by certain people not affiliated with Fender) in recreating certain vintage appointments may add to the practical difficulties confronting a budding "guitar-cheologist" when examining Fender guitars from the '50s and '60s.

As a quick rule of thumb, the neck markings give the better indication of the production year, but they don't specify when an instrument was actually completed and marketed. Whenever available, a certificate of authenticity like the one coming with Custom Shop instruments is the best reference for dating purposes.

NECK DATE

Fender instruments of various vintage are quite often dated at the bottom of the neck where the neck meets the body. By loosening the screws securing the neck to the body, it is usually possible to see a date. Of course, this is not the case on the Custom Shop models built with a set neck.

The date, if any, indicates when the neck was finished rather than the date when the guitar was completed. In fact, neck dates may precede the final assembly by a few weeks or months, and occasionally a few years. It is nonetheless commonly used as the principal reference for dating a Fender because of its availability through the years.

- On the instruments from the early 1950s, the neck date is penciled in black below the truss rod adjusting bolt. Sometimes it may be penciled in green or red. The early dates are very precise as they indicate the month-day-year. For instance:

    10-30-50 (October 30, 1950) on Broadcaster #0115

    11-19-51 (November 19, 1951) on Precision Bass #0212

    5-31-52 (May 31, 1952) on Telecaster #3151

    4-23-53 (April 23, 1953) on Esquire #4551

Until 1955 the date is usually preceded by the initials of the person who shaped the neck, e.g., TG, DZ, XA, AG. The earliest Esquires (one or two-pickup variants) from 1950, as well as some Broadcasters, do not feature any neck date at all.

- At the end of 1953 the mention of the day was dropped from the penciled neck date, which then retained only the month and the year. For instance:

    12-53 (December, 1953) on Telecaster #2289

    6-54 (June, 1954) on Stratocaster #0080

Penciled neck dates were consistently used until March 1962, except for about a year after spring 1959. Neck markings were then temporarily suspended after a customer allegedly complained about an obscene message. The dating process was resumed in 1960.

- In March, 1962, Fender changed to a rubber-stamped neck marking showing the month via its first three letters (JAN = January) and, as before, the year of production by its last two digits (62 = 1962). At first sight, the rubber-stamped marking could suggest that the mention of the day of production was resumed in 1962. For instance:

    1 DEC 62 B on Jaguar #94454

    2 MAY 62 B on Stratocaster #80745

This is not the case, as the numeral displayed before the month is actually a code specific to each Fender model. Given the constant expansion of the Fender range, such reference numbers were probably devised to facilitate production and storage. The main codes found on the necks made between 1962 and 1973 are:

1 = Jaguar (1962 through mid-1966)

2 = Stratocaster (1962 through late 1965)

3 = Telecaster

4 = Jazzmaster (1962 through mid-1966)

5 = Precision Bass

6 = Bass VI

7 = Jazz Bass

8 = Mustang (long scale neck)

9 = Duo-Sonic, Musicmaster, Mustang, Swinger/Musiclander

10 = Coronado I

11 = Bass V

12 = Electric XII, Custom/Maverick

13 = Stratocaster (late 1965 through mid-1968)

14 = Coronado XII

15 = Jaguar (from mid-1966)

16 = Bronco, Mustang, Musicmaster (from 1967)

17 = Mustang Bass, Musicmaster Bass

18 = Coronado Bass

19 = Jazzmaster (from mid-1966), Coronado II

20 = Coronado Bass II

22 = Stratocaster (from mid-1968)

23 = Telecaster Bass

For the record, the letter found after the date is also a code used to indicate the neck width, for instance:

A is narrow (1.500 inch)

B is standard (1.625 inch)

C is wide (1.750 inch)

D is extra wide (1.875 inch)

as optional neck widths were formally offered on certain models by 1960.

In some specific cases, the six-digit numbers from the F-series are a more reliable source of information than the neck markings. This holds true when attempting to date hybrid models like the Custom/Maverick or the Swinger/Musiclander marketed between mid-1969 and 1972. These models with alternative names were designed to use up excess inventory, and as such their neck dates may be totally misleading. For instance:

| | Custom | #244998 with a July, 1966 neck date |
| vs. | Telecaster | #244679 with a May, 1969 neck date |

or

| | Swinger | #271295 with a January, 1967 neck date |
| vs. | Swinger | #271956 with a June, 1969 neck date |

Over the years Fender used various types of neck markings. From top to bottom: 1951, 1953, 1965, 1969, 1972 explicitly, 1972 in coded form, 1988, and 2006.

August, 1951, body date penciled in the neck pocket

November, 1980, tag glued in the neck pocket of a Telecaster with an S8 number

May, 1963, body date penciled in the vibrato back cavity of a Stratocaster

• On some late 1960s and early 1970s instruments, the neck displays a green ink-stamp featuring between seven and nine digits instead of the normal month/year date marking. The first and the last digits seem to conform to the 1960s codes for the model and the neck width. For instance:

3 47 9 9B   on Telecaster Custom #255985

5 458 11 9B   on Precision Bass #277883

22 319 9 9B   on Stratocaster #267917

Further cross-checking suggests that the penultimate digits before the width code could refer to the month/year in numerical form. Thus, in the above examples, 99 would stand for September, 1969, and 119 for November, 1969,. The middle three digits are more difficult to decipher as, prima facie, they do not fit a daily or a weekly count. They could represent a production order number.

• In early 1973 the explicit dating of the neck was (temporarily) suspended and replaced by an entirely new eight-digit marking rubber-stamped in black, blue, or red. For instance:

0901 2823 on a Stratocaster #420592

0103 4253 on a Precision Bass #586817

0701 4542 on a Telecaster Custom #657334

The first group of four digits unmistakably refers to the revised model codes introduced by Fender on the threshold of the 1970s. Thus, in the above examples, 0901 refers to a custom-colored Stratocaster with a rosewood board; 0103 to a custom-colored Precision Bass with a maple neck; 0701 to a custom-finished Telecaster Custom with a rosewood fretboard. The first pair of digits indicates the model basic code, while the second pair specifies the basic appointments in terms of finish, type of neck, tremolo, etc. Sometimes the "0" in front is not inked and, for example, the code reads "9" instead of "09."

The main model codes (first two digits) found in the 1970s are:

01	Precision Bass and Jazzmaster
02	Jazz Bass
03	Telecaster Bass
04	Mustang Bass
05	Bass VI and Jaguar
06	Bass V
07	Musicmaster Bass and Telecaster Custom (second variant)
08	Telecaster Deluxe
09	Stratocaster
13	Telecaster (standard)
14	Telecaster Custom (first variant)
30	Telecaster Thinline
40	Bronco and Starcaster
45	Musicmaster
49	Mustang
50	Custom/Maverick

Given that product codes are shown in abbreviated form on the neck (i.e., four digits instead of six), some models may share the same four-digit reference. Thus 0100 may be found on a sunburst Jazzmaster (full code 11-0100) and a sunburst Precision Bass with a rosewood fretboard (full code 18-0100). Likewise, 0700 may be found on a sunburst Telecaster Custom with a rosewood fretboard (full code 11-0700) and a Musicmaster Bass (full code 18-0700).

The principal codes for the second pair of digits are:

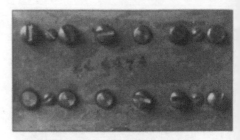

1974 date marking on a Fender humbucking pickup

00	standard finish with a rosewood fretboard
01	custom finish with a rosewood fretboard
02	standard finish with a maple neck
03	custom finish with a maple neck

(Note: 2 simply replaces 0 on left-handed models.)

The second group of four digits has yet to be fully deciphered—or confirmed by Fender old-timers! The cross-checking of several neck codes suggests that the penultimate digit would indicate the year of manufacture of the neck, while the first two digits could refer to the week in the year, as used in the codes applied to potentiometers (see below). This would work out as follows:

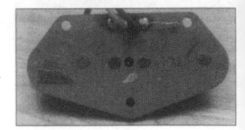

- 0901 2823 is on a Stratocaster neck from 1972 (28th week)

- 0103 4253 is on a Precision Bass neck from 1975 (42nd week)

- 0701 4542 is on a Telecaster Custom neck from 1974 (45th week)

Telecaster bridge pickup with a 1967 date marking

This interpretation seems to work in about 90 percent of the guitars, but as usual with Fender, there may be a few cases where the serial number and the neck date seem to be two or even three years apart. Having said that, some necks may be without any codes while others such as the Telecaster Deluxe introduced in 1973 read "TEL-DELX.73."

- By 1981 the eight-digit inventory code used during the 1970s was deleted and the explicit dating of the neck was reinstated. On the standard models from the early 1980s, it is usually ink-stamped in black numerals with a month/day/year format on the heel, and often also on an inspection tag (sometimes without the day) glued on the underside of the neck. For instance:

    12 19 81 (tag) on Telecaster #S8850740

    9 2 82 (heel) on Stratocaster #E207783

    10 14 83 on vintage '52 Telecaster #4720

December, 1981, inspection tag glued on the underside of the neck heel

- By 1983 the format of the date marking was slightly changed, and the month was shown with three letters instead of numerals. This is the main style in use today, with black or red ink on the regular production models. For instance:

    OCT 12 1983 on Elite Telecaster #E316667

    JUL 13 1998 on American Std. Stratocaster #N8338206

    MAR 31 2006 on Vintage Telecaster Custom #V153294

- A dated inspection tag may also be glued on the underside of the neck, thereby giving two slightly different date markings per neck on some instruments. For instance:

    SEP 16 1998 (heel) on Tele-Sonic #N8346433

    and

    OCT 02 1998 (tag)

The 137825 marking on this CTS pot indicates that it was made during the 25th week of 1958.

The early pre-Time Machine Relic models aged by Vince Cunetto from 1995 up to mid-1999 have necks stamped on the underside of the heel with a specific six-digit code reading YDDDxx. For instance: 824516 means 245th day of 1998. The Time Machine models produced by the Custom Shop since 1999 have regular Fender neck stamps, e.g., Jan 09 2005 on a Nocaster with #R3999.

It should be noted, however, that the date marking found on a Custom Shop neck may be at variance by more than a year with the (later) date mentioned on the certificate of authenticity coming with the instrument (and/or with the body date; see below).

BODY DATE

From late 1950 until late 1963, Fender bodies were also fairly consistently dated, either in the neck pocket or in a pickup routing. On the Stratocaster the body date is frequently found in the vibrato cavity routed in the back. However, since the date was penciled on before the body was finished, it may not show on certain instruments because of their opaque color.

The body date (if any) was penciled with numerals indicating the month/day/year until late 1953, and thereafter only the month/year. For instance:

10/18/51 on Telecaster #1201 (neck date: 10/20/51)

3/5/53 on Esquire #3482 (neck date: 2/16/53)

After late 1953 the day was dropped from the body date as it was dropped from the neck date. For instance:

4/54 on Telecaster #4593 (neck date: 4/54)

10/63 on Stratocaster #L11081 (neck date: SEP 63)

Depending on the (original) popularity of the models and their finishes, neck and body dates may be identical or differ by a few months. When the dating of necks was suspended in spring 1959, body dates were maintained, and they can help in assessing the vintage of an instrument made during that period. For instance:

5/59 on Telecaster Custom #38820 (no neck date)

11/59 on Stratocaster #48373 (no neck date)

On the instruments made after 1963 a body date is no longer visible, regardless of the finish. One can only assume that the procedure was altogether discontinued in the mid-'60s. Coincidentally, 1964 is the year when date markings began to appear on the bottom plate of most pickups.

Body dates reappeared on the threshold of the 1980s. At first they were either penciled or rubber-stamped on a paper label glued inside the neck pocket. Unlike the dates from the '50s and early '60s, they refer to a post-finish quality check rather than the date at which the raw body was shaped. For instance:

11 20 80 on Telecaster #S838365

11 16 81 on Stratocaster #S991370

In the above cases, the diligent reader will notice that the dates are not in synch with the vintage suggested by the serial numbers.

Since the 1990s body dates have adopted the same format as neck dates or come in the form of a fraction such as 05/06 (for May, 2006) ink-stamped in the neck pocket. It is not unusual for a body date to be at variance by several months, if not a year or more, with the neck date of the same instrument. In particular, Custom Shop models may routinely feature neck and body dates that vary by one year, and that are not aligned with the date mentioned on the certificate of authenticity, which is logically the most recent date of them all.

PICKUP DATE

On the threshold of 1964 Fender began to mention a date on the bottom plate of most of its pickups (among the exceptions were Telecaster guitars with their narrow front pickup). These dates indicate when the pickup was completed or tested before storage, and not when the instrument was finished.

On guitars and basses made during the 1960s and 1970s the following types of markings may be found:

- on the pickups with a bottom plate made of black fiber, the date is usually rubber-stamped with yellow ink (e.g., FEB 10 64)

- on the light grey bottom plates introduced in mid-1964, the date is usually penciled or handwritten in black with a thick grease pen or felt pen (e.g., 10-25-67)

- on the dark grey bottom plates introduced in the late '60s, the date in clear is replaced by a three- to six-digit code, rubber-stamped in black or red, which may be deciphered to indicate the year. As a quick rule of thumb, the last digit(s) refers to the year.

The following pickup dates come from at least one of the pickups of the guitars listed:

JAN 11 64 (1964) on Stratocaster #L26531

10-6-65 (1965) on Jazzmaster #L90400

8-26-66 (1966) on Musicmaster #146956

11-6-67 (1967) on Bronco #210398

2-5-68 (1968) on Mustang Bass #210424

52 9 (1969) on Telecaster #395620

222 70 (1970) on Jazz Bass #279506

510 71 (1971) on Precision Bass #305881

17 51 72 (1972) on Stratocaster #382999

479 73 (1973) on Telecaster #395620

1405 74 (1974) on Stratocaster #528763

9 23 75 (1975) on Telecaster #585393

6 14 76 (1976) on Stratocaster #7668076

122 77 (1977) on Stratocaster #S771614

77 31 78 (1978) on Jazz Bass #S843968

By the 1980s Fender was using one-piece moulded bobbins made of black plastic, which do not feature any marking other than the part reference number.

PICKUP HARNESS DATE

Besides the neck and body, the very early Fender electrics usually feature a third date penciled on a piece of masking tape located in the controls cavity. During the years 1953 to 1955, the piece of tape also mentions the first name (Mary, Gloria, Virginia, etc.) of the woman who did the job. For instance:

• 8/20/51 on Nocaster #1924 (neck: 8/8/51)

• Gloria 8/26/53 on Telecaster #3849 (neck: 8/23/53)

• Virginia 10/28/54 on Stratocaster #0080 (neck: 6-54)

• Mary 9/13/55 on Stratocaster #6883 (neck: 9-55)

After 1955 this date usually ceased to appear, but it is certainly the most accessible date to log an early Fender electric precisely.

POT SOURCE CODE

The potentiometers used on electrics (whether Fender, Gibson, or Gretsch) usually feature a date-coded reference stamped on the top or side of the shell. Depending on the period, this code features six or seven digits reading CCCYWW or CCCYYWW, in which:

• CCC indicates the manufacturer's source code

• Y or YY shows the year of production of the potentiometer

• WW shows the week of production in the year (01 to 52)

For example: a potentiometer on Esquire #29643 (neck date: 9-58) is stamped with 3596 250K AUDIO 137825 in which 137825 indicates that this potentiometer was made:

• by CTS Corporation (code = 137)

• June, 1958)

In theory the above number could also apply to a pot made in 1948, but 1940s pots are often not coded, or their code may be ink-stamped in blue or black rather than impressed into the shell. In any case, choosing a decade for six-digit pot codes is a matter of judgement. This choice no longer exists with the seven-digit codes introduced in the early 1960s, where the year is shown with two digits. For example, a potentiometer on Telecaster #605659 (no neck date) is impressed with 015479 1MEG AUDIO 3047414, in which the latter reference indicates that this pot was made:

• by Stackpole Electronics (code = 304)

• during the 14th week of 1974 (April, 1974)

Provided the potentiometer is an original part and it has not been replaced, the date implied by the source code indicates the earliest possible year when an instrument could have been made. Conversely, pots are often purchased in high volumes, and it may take a few years to absorb a big order. For example, most of the Fender electrics from 1966–1969 feature pots made in 1966. The date suggested by the source code on potentiometers may be useful primarily to support the dating of 1970s Fender electrics, and more generally of any instrument without a readily available neck or body date.

For the record, the manufacturer's source code is assigned by the Electronic Industries Association and is marked on all the products (pots, capacitors, resistors, fuses, switches, loudspeakers, etc.) made by a registered manufacturer. On Fender instruments, the most commonly-found codes and manufacturers are:

137: CTS Corporation

140: Clarostat Manufacturing Co.

304: Stackpole Electronics

1955 Precision Bass

1951 "No-Caster" transition model between the Broadcaster and the Telecaster with no name but Fender on the headstock

Rare 1967 Telecaster Custom with body bound in black and separate maple fingerboard. Note the lack of a dark spot above the nut.

1957 Stratocaster with single-ply white pickguard

1965 12-string electric

1969 Custom guitar made from 12-string Electric left-over parts after the model was discontinued

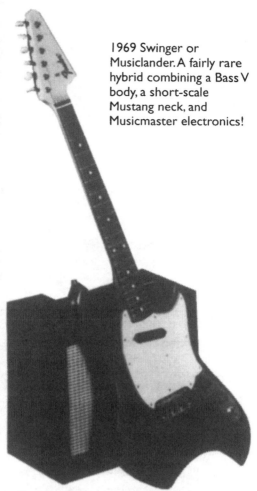

1969 Swinger or Musiclander. A fairly rare hybrid combining a Bass V body, a short-scale Mustang neck, and Musicmaster electronics!

1965 Bass V, the first solid-body electric bass with five strings

1960 Jazzmaster with anodized pickguard

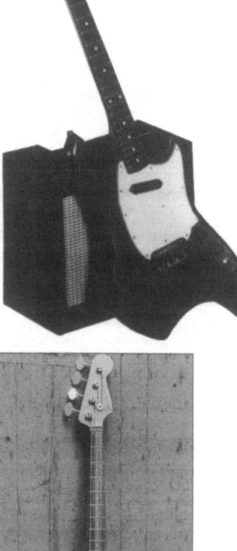

1960 Jazz Bass, with concentric (or stacked) knobs and unbound fretboard

1966 Precision Bass

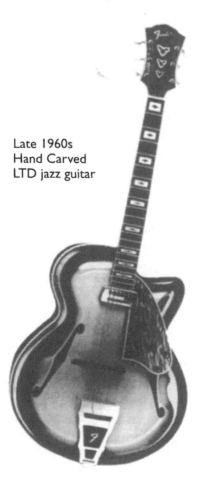

Late 1960s Hand Carved LTD jazz guitar

Orville Gibson (1856–1918) started making stringed instruments in the latter part of the 19th century. A few years after launching his business in Kalamazoo, Michigan, he signed an agreement with local investors that led to the foundation of the Gibson Mandolin-Guitar Mfg. Co. in 1902. In the early part of the century the factory produced mainly mandolins, but during the 1920s they were gradually superseded by banjos and guitars.

With the inception of electric guitars in the 1930s and their growing popularity after WWII, Gibson became the world's leading manufacturer of professional grade guitars of all types. In late 1969 the business—owned since 1944 by Chicago Musical Instruments—was acquired by ECL Industries. The new owner later changed its name to Norlin and presided over what is widely perceived as a period of decline for Gibson.

In 1974 guitar production was split between Kalamazoo and a new factory in Nashville. The Kalamazoo plant closed down in the fall of 1984, shortly before Norlin disposed of Gibson. In January, 1986, the business was purchased by a group of investors headed by Henry Juszkiewicz and David Berryman, who have re-established the brand's credentials. The new owners then acquired the Flatiron mandolin company based in Bozeman, Montana, which, in 1989, became the home of Gibson flat-top guitars. More recently, a third facility has been opened in Memphis, Tennessee, and has been assigned the production of thinline electrics like the ES-335, while the Nashville plant continues to make all solid-bodies.

FOREWORD ON GIBSON NUMBERS

Many numbering schemes have been used since 1903 to register Gibson guitars depending on the periods and the models. As a result, dating a Gibson by its identification number(s) is sometimes tricky, and great care should be exerted to avoid any misconception. Numbers can be found in a variety of patterns and formats throughout the years. Some of them are date-coded while others are part of some consecutive series.

Gibson numbers can be split in two broad categories: the true serial numbers and the factory order numbers (FON). FON were concurrently used with serial numbers until early 1961 to monitor production schedules within the plant. For practical purposes, this means that the pre-1961 upper-grade models (e.g., Super 400, L-5, J-200, Byrdland) usually feature two distinct numbers, whereas the lower-grade ones (e.g., L-50, ES-125, J-45, LG-1) only have a single factory order number.

Some of the instruments made between 1942 and 1949 may not carry any visible number at all. Consequently their vintage can only be assessed on the basis of their detailed specifications. Likewise, the first Les Paul model was issued in 1952 without any visible number before a fresh approach to solid-body numbers was devised in 1953.

From 1975 date-coded serial numbers were enforced on all production models. Like its main competitors, however, Gibson has spawned a vast array of historic reissues and special editions that often feature bespoke numbers. This section describes the various schemes used on Gibson guitars since 1903 and comments on their usefulness for dating purposes. Remember that the meaning of a number depends not only on its format (letters/numerals), but also on where and how it is applied.

THE ORIGINAL SERIES: 1903–1947

The earliest instruments from the Gibson Mandolin-Guitar Mfg. Co. do not feature any serial number on the label glued inside the body. The first mention of a number appeared in 1903, but it took until about 1908 before the model name was added to the label.

Style and Location

The original series ran from 1903 until 1947. It features four- and then five-digit numbers issued on a consecutive basis, and progressively ranging from #1000 up to #99,999 (assigned to an L-7 archtop guitar on April 28, 1947).

Until about 1933 the numbers were penciled or hand-inked on a white oval paper label glued on the inside of the back, beneath the round soundhole or the upper f-hole. Between 1933 and 1947 the numbers were no longer penciled, but were usually ink-stamped. The early labels from the 1902–1903 period have an inset photo of Orville Gibson with a lyre, which was dropped around 1908. In the early 1930s the company's name was modified to Gibson Inc. (no more Mandolin-Guitar).

Two variants of the standard paper label are worth mentioning:

- the Gibson Master Model label introduced in late 1922 on the style 5 line of instruments designed by Lloyd Loar and used until about 1927;

- the circular labels used between 1918 and 1926 on the Army and Navy instruments, and then on the Junior models.

Comments on Usefulness

The dating chart shown in table A has been put together using information from various sources. It takes advantage of the research by Gruhn/Carter on the early years and of the fine-tuning done by this author on 1930s and 1940s numbers after consulting the available factory ledgers. Overall this chart is reasonably accurate and it enables an instrument to be logged with a one-year tolerance.

It is interesting to note that the numbers were used up fairly rapidly and consistently until the mid-1920s, but then took some time to reach the 99,999 mark in 1947. This can be explained by the distinct schemes enforced by Gibson for each type of fretted instrument. By the time Gibson flat-top acoustics debuted in 1926, the original five-digit serial numbers were only applied to the higher-priced models, while lower-grade ones kept only a factory order number (see page 32). As a result, many 1930s and 1940s instruments are outside the scope of the original series.

In addition, many instruments released after WWII do not carry a serial number or even a (visible) factory order number. Therefore their dating can only be achieved on the strength of their specifications.

The Master models (e.g., L-5 guitar) produced between June 1922 and December 1924 carry a second label beneath the lower f-hole, signed by engineer Lloyd Loar with the date the instrument was approved. For instance:

- F-5 with #73993 signed on July 9, 1923
- L-5 with #79621 signed on December 1, 1924

1940 serial number (96520) on a white oval label

Artist serial number (A32831) from February 1960

1964 serial number (199123) impressed into the peghead

1941 FON (2507G38) on the inside back

1939 FON (EGE-4551) impressed into the peghead

1959 FON (S9985 30) rubber-stamped on the inside back

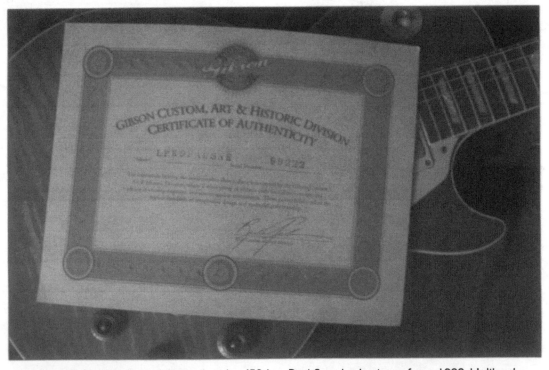

Certificate of authenticity delivered with a '59 Les Paul Standard reissue from 1999. Unlike the certificates issued by Fender, CoA from Gibson are not usually dated, presumably because the serial number is date-coded (MYxxx).

1958 (8 xxxx) inked-on number

Eight-digit number from 1976 with a 00 prefix

2006 inked-on number on Historic Collection Les Paul Junior (double cutaway with TV finish, model code 8)

Custom Shop inked-on number from 2006 (CS6xxxx)

2006 impressed number on early 1960s SG Special reissue (model code 1)

Eight-digit number from 1982 (8xxx2xxx)

Newly expanded nine-digit number on 2006 regular model

TABLE A   ORIGINAL SERIES 1903–1947

Year	Lowest No.	Highest No.	Year	Lowest No.	Highest No.	Year	Lowest No.	Highest No.
1903	1000	1500	1919	47900	53800	1935	92300	92800
1904	1500	2500	1920	53800	63650	1936	92800	94000
1905	2500	3500	1921	63650	69300	1937	94000	95000
1906	3500	5500	1922	69300	71400	1938	95000	95500
1907	5500	8300	1923	71400	74900	1939	95500	96000
1908	8300	9700	1924	74900	81200			(also EA5000s)
1909	9700	10100	1925	81200	82700	1940	96000	96600
1910	10100	10600	1926	82700	83600			(also FA5000s)
1911	10600	10850	1927	83600	85400	1941	96600	97300
1912	10850	13350	1928	85400	87300	1942	97300	97600
1913	13350	16100	1929	87300	89750	1943	97600	97800
1914	16100	20150	1930	89750	90200	1944	97800	98150
1915	20150	25150	1931	90200	90450	1945	98150	98600
1916	25150	32000	1932	90450	90700	1946	98600	99328
1917	32000	39500	1933	90700	91400	1947	99329	99999*
1918	39500	47900	1934	91400	92300	* L-7 registered on April 28		

PRE-WAR ARTIST NUMBERS: 1938–1940

Style and Location

Another type of serial number was used concurrently with the original series in 1938 and 1940. It is characterized by a two-letter prefix, i.e.:

- DA = 1938
- EA = 1939
- FA = 1940

and is rubber-stamped on a paper label or sometimes impressed as well on the back of the headstock.

The second letter indicates that these numbers were exclusively applied to what Gibson then called the "Artist" models (e.g., Super 400, L-5, ES-250). The four numerals after the prefix progressed from 5000s to 5100s in 1938, 5000s to 5600s in 1939, and from 5000s to 5100s in early 1940. By spring 1940 pre-war Artist numbers were phased out.

Comments on Usefulness

The pre-war Artist numbers are date-coded and therefore reliable for logging the year of issue of an instrument.

POST-WAR ARTIST NUMBERS: 1947–1961

Style and Location

When the original series reached #99,999 in spring, 1947, Gibson did not carry forward the scheme with numbers in the 100,000s. Instead the company started a fresh series preceded by the letter A (again for Artist models). The first number was A100 on April 28, 1947, with the following numbers progressing consecutively through three, four, and then five digits. The final number was A36147 recorded on February 21, 1961.

Between April, 1947, and January, 1955, the Artist numbers were rubber-stamped on white oval labels. In January, 1955, Gibson first used pre-numbered orange oval labels, on which only the style and the type of the instrument were filled in. According to factory ledgers, the first orange label came out with #A20001 and was registered on January 13, 1955. In the process, #A18751 through #A20000 were written off and not applied to any instrument. Artist numbers can be found on all the upper-grade models produced between 1947 and 1961, whether acoustics or electrics.

Year/Month	1st No.	Date	Model	Year/Month	1st No.	Date	Model
1947	A100	April 28	L-7 (first #)	1955	A18668 +	January 6	ES-295
	A411	July 2	L-7		A20468	April 4	L-5
	A813	October 1	L-5P		A20991	July 1	ES-175N
1948	A1305	January 8	L-12P		A21356	October 5	Custom Classic
	A1540	April 1	L-7N	1956	A21910	January 6	L-7C
	A1849	July 2	L-5		A22556	April 4	ES-175DN
	A2369	October 6	Super 400		A23387	July 3	J-200
1949	A2666	January 5	L-7		A24135	October 2	Super 400CES
	A2999	April 1	L-7	1957	A24756	January 3	L-7C
	A3353	July 1	ES-350		A25368	April 4	J-200
	A3749	October 3	ES-175		A25899	July 3	ES-5 S.M.
1950	A4414	January 3	ES-175		A26381	October 4	J-185
	A5012	April 3	L-7CN	1958	A26820	January 6	ES-5 S.M.
	A5456	July 3	L-7		A27361	April 2	J-200
	A5833	October 2	ES-175		A27816	July 1	Super 400CES
1951	A6598	January 4	ES-175N		A28282	October 3	Super 400CES
	A7237	April 3	L-4C	1959	A28881	January 9	J-200
	A8030	July 2	ES-350		A29532	April 1	ES-335T
	A8705	October 1	L-4C		A30569	July 13	EB-2
1952	A9420	January 2	Super 400CES		A31281	October 1	ES-355T
	A10111	April 2	J-185	1960	A32285	January 4	ES-335T
	A11057	July 1	ES-175		A33140	April 4	ES-345T
	A11680	October 2	J-185		A34068	July 1	J-200
1953	A12463	January 8	J-185		A34659	October 3	ES-175
	A13213	April 1	F-5	1961	A35646	January 3	Hummingbird
	A14332	July 1	ES-175		A36147	February 21	L-5CES (last #)
	A15432	October 1	J-185				
1954	A16102	January 5	L-5C				
	A16761	April 5	SJ-200				
	A17435	July 1	J-200				
	A18149	October 4	ES-5				

+ #A18751 through #A20000 were written off in factory ledgers

Comments on Usefulness

The dating chart shown in table B was compiled after using the two factory ledgers where all the Artist numbers were neatly registered on a daily basis. It shows the first number used at the beginning of each quarter between 1947 and 1961, with the actual date of registration.

SOLID-BODIES' NUMBERS: 1953–1961

When the goldtop Les Paul model was premiered in 1952, it was not deemed necessary to apply any number on it. In 1953 a specific scheme was devised for solid-bodies and applied to Spanish as well as Hawaiian electrics. (Note: Pre-war Hawaiian lap-steels usually carry a factory order number impressed in the wood, but not the post-war models.)

SOLID-BODY NUMBERS 1953–1961
Basic patterns

Year	Pattern	Year	Pattern	Year	Pattern	Year	Pattern
1953	3 xxxx	1956	6 xxxx	1959	9 xxxx	1960	0 xxxx
1954	4 xxxx		61xxxx		91xxxx		01xxxx
1955	5 xxxx	1957	7 xxxx		92xxxx	1961	1 xxxx
	51xxxx	1958	8 xxxx		93xxxx		

Style and Location

The scheme introduced in 1953 consists of a five- to six-digit number, ink-stamped on the back of the peghead. The first numeral, slightly apart from the others, shows the year of production while the remaining numerals were allotted on a roughly cumulative basis, hence a basic Y xxxx format. For instance:

- Les Paul Model   #3 0915 (1953)
- Electric Bass   #4 0239 (1954)

There is no hyphen between the first and second numerals but, as a practical convention, one is usually inserted when putting this type of number on paper. These date-coded numbers were used from 1953 until early 1961. According to factory records, the latest number assigned would be #1-1075 recorded on February 24, 1961 for a (single cutaway) Les Paul Custom.

At first Gibson used black ink to rubber-stamp numbers on its solid-bodies. However, with the inception of the Les Paul Custom in 1954 came yellow-inked numbers on instruments with a dark finish. Meanwhile, the earliest Les Paul Customs were released without any visible number or sometimes with a tiny three-digit number impressed on the top edge of the headstock.

By late 1955 six-digit numbers (with an extra numeral right after the digit for the year) were introduced into the scheme. In fact, the factory (wrongly) used the numbers accrued at the end of 1954 in 1955, instead of starting afresh with 5-0001. Thus a Les Paul Junior #4-4863 was entered on December 23, 1954, while another Junior #5-5291 was recorded on February 3, 1955. As a result, higher six-digit numbers were eventually used at the end of 1955, e.g., Les Paul Model #513578.

Six-digit numbers can also be found, albeit more logically in terms of production output, at the end of 1956, 1959, and 1960. Incidentally, for some reason, inked-on numbers from 1959 can go as high as the 933,000s, usually on Les Paul Juniors.

Comments on Usefulness

The chart shown in table C reproduces the various patterns of the inked-on numbers found on solid-bodies between 1953 and 1961. However, it should be noted that the date suggested may not correspond to the actual date of shipment from the factory. For example, several Les Paul Juniors ¾ carrying 1959 numbers were shipped only in 1961. Likewise, a few Flying Vs and Explorers carrying 1958 and 1959 numbers were issued in the early '60s.

FACTORY ORDER NUMBERS: 1935–1961

In the old days Gibson guitars were generally produced in racks or batches of 35 to 40 units, occasionally more if the model was very popular. A factory order number (FON hereafter)—also called factory work order—was assigned to each batch in production, and each instrument in the batch was in turn ranked at an early stage in the manufacturing process.

FONs usually show up on most guitars until early 1961, although they are barely visible sometimes. They are rubber-stamped or inked-on inside the body, either on the neck block or on the back. FONs are quite useful because they may be the only way to precisely assess the vintage of instruments that do not carry any serial number.

Additionally, FONs may be used to cross-check the dating suggested by the serial number of upper-grade models, which until 1961 usually have TWO identification numbers. The FON always suggests an earlier vintage than the serial number (if any) because it was applied at an earlier stage in the manufacturing process. For instance, an ES-5SM carrying a 1955 FON (W3205-2) is registered with a March, 1956 serial number (A22303).

Regrettably, the early FONs used by Gibson up to the mid-'30s do not lend themselves to the formation of a neat dating chart. They are not date-coded and, although the numbers were probably allocated on a roughly cumulative basis, it is difficult to group them convincingly with an annual cut-off in the absence of available factory documentation.

Alphabetical FON: 1935–1942

Style and Location

In 1935 a code letter relating to the year of manufacture was inserted in the FON, beginning with letter A for 1935, then B for 1936, etc. This scheme was discontinued in early 1942 with letter H. Depending on the period, the alphabetical FON may be found in different styles and locations:

- During the period 1935–1938 the FON was ink-stamped inside the body, either on the neck block (flat-tops) or beneath the lower *f*-hole (other hollow bodies). The batch number and the letter were stamped with black or blue ink while the individual suffix was penciled in red or black. For instance:

  L-50 with 273 A 22 (1935)
  L-4 #93876 with 1026 B 5 (1936)
  ES-150 with 440 C 10 (1937)
  L-12 #95339 with 330 D 8 (1938)

- Beginning in mid-1938, the FON of lower-grade models was no longer rubber-stamped on the neck block or on the back, but impressed into the wood on the back of the peghead. In the process, the format was also amended with the code letter for the year relocated as a prefix, with one or two extra letters added right behind it. Moreover, there was no longer an added suffix per instrument as each one received a distinct number. For instance:

  ES-150 with DG-2254 (1938)
  ES-150 with DGE5429 (1938)
  ES-100 with EGE-4754 (1939)
  L-0 with EG-6219 (1939)
  ES-100 with FGE2264 (1940)
  L-50 with FG-2750 (1940)

As shown above, the code letter is followed by either G (for Gibson) or GE (for Gibson Electric, albeit inconsistently), but also by K (on the low-budget Kalamazoo-branded models) or W (for the Recording King instruments made for Montgomery Ward).

TABLE D

FACTORY ORDER NUMBERS 1935–1961

Pre-War FON Code Letters 1935–1942

Year	Code Letter
1935	A
1936	B
1937	C
1938	D
1939	E
1940	F
1941	G
1942	H

Post-War Consecutive FON 1949–1952

Year	FON series
1949	100s through 1000s to low 2000s
1950	high 2000s through 3000s, 4000s, low 5000s
1951	high 5000s through 6000s, 7000s, 8000s, low 9000s
1952	high 9000s

Post-War FON Code Letters 1952–1961

Year	Code Letter
1952	Z
1953	Y
1954	X
1955	W
1956	V
1957	U
1958	T
1959	S
1960	R
1961	Q

Meanwhile, upper-grade models from the period 1938–1940 continued to use the previous style of inked-on FON. For instance:

- L-5N #EA5582 with 603 E 1 (1939)
- ES-300 #96520 with 1931 F 24 (1940)

- In 1940 FONs impressed on the headstock were phased out, and they were again ink-stamped inside the body on all the guitars, regardless of their status. For instance:

- ES-150 (no SN) with 552 F 9 (1940)
- ES-300 #96885 with 2584 G 17 (1941)
- ES-125 (no SN) with 7200 H 11 (1942)

Comments on Usefulness

The alphabetical FON can be used to reliably date the instruments made during the 1935–1941 period. On upper-grade models the FON may suggest an earlier vintage than the serial number featured on the paper label. This is normal given their respective role in the manufacturing process.

War Period and Early Post-War FONs: 1942–1948

Some form of batch numbering continued to be used during the 1942–1948 period, but it is very difficult to align these FONs into a meaningful pattern. For instance, the following generic batch series can be found on guitars made between 1942 and 1945:

- 300s, 500s, 800s, 900s, 1000s
- 2000s, 2100s, 2200s, 2300s, 2400s, 2500s, 2600s, 2700s, 2800s, 2900s
- 4400s, 4500s, 4600s

It is, however, difficult to assign them categorically on a year-by-year basis unless one refers to the specific models carrying them. For example, FONs 910 and 2005 were both used on the earliest SJ flat-tops from 1942 while FON 301 was used subsequently on LG-2 made in 1943 and 1944.

FONs were inconsistently assigned after WWII, and many post-war models do not feature any number at all. For instance, 1947 instruments typically show no factory order number.

Visible FON allocation reappeared in 1948 on some high-end models without proper serial numbers (e.g., ES-300) as well as on acoustics carrying an A-prefixed serial number (see page 30). Batch numbers in the 2000s, 3000s, and 4000s can thus be found on certain guitars made in 1948 and early 1949. These 1948–1949 FONs are inked on and consist of two parts: a four-batch number followed by a one- or two-digit suffix. Like the 1942–1945 FONs, they are not date-coded. It is not until later in 1949 that FONs were again assigned consistently to all the Gibson models.

Post-War Consecutive FONs: 1949–1952

Style and Location

The instruments made between 1949 and early 1952 carry a rubber-stamped FON on the neck block or on the back. These post-war FONs consist of a basic three- to four-digit number running from #100 to #9999, completed by a one- or two-digit suffix to rank each instrument.

The 1949–1952 FONs are similar in format to the numbers issued during the 1942–1945 period, but two points help distinguish them:

1. The individual suffix number of the FON is rubber-stamped in the 1949–1952 numbers, whereas it is penciled (often in red) in the 1942–1945 numbers.

2. The 1949–1952 instruments feature the modern Gibson logo on the headstock, whereas the 1942–1945 ones sport the old Gibson script.

Comments on Usefulness

The dating chart shown in table D was put together after consulting available factory records and cross-checking many instruments from the period 1949–1952. It is therefore considered reliable for dating purposes.

Reverse Alphabetical FONs: 1952–1961

Style and Location

In early 1952 Gibson went back to a date-coded scheme. As was already the case in the 1930s, a letter relating to the year of manufacture was inserted in the FON, which otherwise kept the same basic format. This time, however, the scheme started backwards through the alphabet, and the first letter used in 1952 was Z, followed by Y in 1953, etc. The series came to a halt in early 1961 with letter Q, which is fairly rare.

Concurrently with the annual alphabet countdown, batch numbers continued to be allotted on a consecutive basis, moving from #100 through to #9999 and then back to #100. Thus, batch #9999 was successively attained in late 1954, mid-1957, and mid-1959.

Comments on Usefulness

Like their pre-war counterparts, the reverse alphabetical FONs are reliable for logging the year of issue of 1952–1961 instruments. This is particularly convenient for lower-grade models without a serial number such as the J-45/50, ES-125, L-50, LG-1, J-160E, etc. For the upper-grade models from that period, it is advisable to use the Artist serial numbers, which give a more precise date of issue.

During a transition period that took place in early 1961, some FONs were used as real serial numbers on a few upper-grade models. On these instruments, what looks like a 1959 or 1960 FON is actually rubber-stamped on the orange oval label inside the body. For instance:

- L-5CES with #S8939 5 registered on February 24, 1961
- ES-5 SM with #R5800 19 registered on June 20, 1961

IMPRESSED SERIAL NUMBERS: 1961–1975

In early 1961 all the prevailing identification numbers (Artist, inked-on numbers, and FONs) were phased out and a common serialization scheme was implemented on ALL the fretted instruments made in Kalamazoo (including Epiphone).

Style and Location

The common scheme introduced in 1961 consists of three- to six-digit numbers systematically impressed into the back of the headstock for greater visibility. According to factory ledgers, the transition between old and new schemes took place mostly between February and March, 1961, a period that saw the same models registered with both old- and new-style numbers. For instance:

- ES-345TD #A35646 (old) on February 1
- ES-345TD #7175 (new) on February 27
- Les Paul Jr #1-0808 (old) on March 13
- Les Paul Jr #3400 (new) on February 24

For the record, the instrument with the lowest number—a classical C-6 with #100—was not registered until May 11, 1961. After quickly progressing through three, four, and five digits between 1961 and 1962, six-digit numbers became the norm from 1963 until 1975. The impressed numbers that debuted in 1961 are not date-coded, and they were assigned on a very rough consecutive basis.

TABLE E — IMPRESSED HEADSTOCK NUMBERS 1961–1969
Main sequences of numbers with corresponding years

Sequence	1961	1962	1963	1964	1965	1966	1967	1968
100 – 41199	1961							
41200 – 61180		1962						
61450 – 64222			1963					
64240 – 71040				1964				
71041 – 71178		1962		1964				
71180 – 95846		1962						
95849 – 99999			1963					
000001 – 008009							1967	
010000 – 042899							1967	
044000 – 044100							1967	
050000 – 054400							1967	
055000 – 070909							1967	
090000 – 099999							1967	
100000 – 106099			1963				1967	
106100 – 108999			1963					
109000 – 109999			1963				1967	
110000 – 111549			1963					
111550 – 115799			1963				1967	
115800 – 118299			1963					
118300 – 120999			1963				1967	
121000 – 139999			1963					
140000 – 140100			1963				1967	
140101 – 144304			1963					
144305 – 144380			1963	1964				
144381 – 145000			1963					
147001 – 149891			1963	1964				
149892 – 152989			1963					
152990 – 174222				1964				
174223 – 179098				1964	1965			
179099 – 199999				1964				
200000 – 250199				1964				
250540 – 290998					1965			
300000 – 305999					1965			
306000 – 306099					1965		1967	
307000 – 307984					1965			
309653 – 310999					1965		1967	
311000 – 320149					1965			
320150 – 320699							1967	
320700 – 325999					1965			
326000 – 326999					1965	1966		
327000 – 329999					1965			
330000 – 330999					1965		1967	1968
331000 – 346119					1965			
346120 – 347099					1965	1966		
348000 – 349100						1966		
349101 – 368639					1965			
368640 – 369890						1966		
370000 – 370999							1967	1968
380000 – 380999						1966	1967	1968
381000 – 385309						1966		
390000 – 390998							1967	
400001 – 400999					1965	1966	1967	1968
401000 – 408699						1966		
408800 – 409670						1966	1967	1968
410000 – 438922						1966		

TABLE E — IMPRESSED HEADSTOCK NUMBERS 1961–1969
Main sequences of numbers with corresponding years

Sequence	1965	1966	1967	1968	1969
500000 – 500999	1965	1966	1967	1968	
501009 – 501600	1965				
501601 – 501702				1968	
501703 – 502706	1965			1968	
503010 – 503109				1968	
503405 – 515499	1965			1968	
515500 – 518120	1965	1966		1968	
518121 – 520955	1965			1968	
520956 – 530050				1968	
530061 – 530469		1966			
530470 – 530850		1966		1968	1969
530851 – 530993				1968	1969
530994 – 539999					1969
540000 – 540795		1966			1969
540796 – 544095					1969
547001 – 547499				1968	
550000 – 556909		1966			
558012 – 567800					1969
570099 – 570755		1966			
580000 – 580999		1966			1969
600000 – 600999		1966	1967	1968	1969
601000 – 601090					1969
605901 – 606090					1969
700000 – 700999		1966	1967	1968	
750000 – 750999				1968	1969
800000 – 800999		1966	1967	1968	1969
801000 – 801999		1966	1967		
802000 – 803999		1966			
804000 – 804999		1966	1967		1969
805000 – 809999		1966			1969
810000 – 810999		1966	1967		1969
811000 – 812838		1966			1969
812900 – 819999					1969
820000 – 820999		1966			1969
821000 – 823830		1966			
824000 – 828999					1969
829000 – 829999		1966			1969
830000 – 830999		1966	1967		1969
831000 – 837999					1969
840000 – 847498		1966	1967		1969
847499 – 848999		1966	1967		
849000 – 849999		1966	1967	1968	
850000 – 850999		1966		1968	
851000 – 858999		1966			
859001 – 891999			1967		
892000 – 892999			1967	1968	
893000 – 895499			1967		
895500 – 895999				1968	
896000 – 896999				1968	1969
897000 – 898999			1967		
899000 – 899999				1968	
900000 – 900999		1966	1967	1968	
901000 – 902250				1968	
903000 – 920899				1968	
940000 – 942999				1968	
945000 – 956999				1968	
959000 – 960909				1968	
970000 – 982178				1968	

On the higher-grade models the numbers were also marked on the paper label glued inside the body beneath the upper f-hole. Beginning in 1970, however, the orange oval label in use since 1955 was superseded by rectangular labels without any mention of the serial number. Otherwise, some numbers may be impressed with slightly taller digits than normal, and experimental models may display an X prefix.

Comments on Usefulness

Impressed serial numbers from 1961–1975 are arguably the least helpful system for dating a Gibson guitar! They are not date-coded and, unlike the 1950s A numbers, they were not always neatly recorded in factory ledgers. When production reached unprecedented peaks during the 1960s, it became increasingly difficult to keep track of every instrument in an orderly fashion, particularly with manual entries in the ledgers. Some numbers look as if they were used at random while others were duplicated.

The duplication syndrome affects most of the 1963 to 1975 numbers. In other words, for various reasons, including a faulty stamping machine, the same serial number can be found on up to ten different instruments of distinct vintage! The greatest care should therefore be exerted when attempting to date a Gibson from that period exclusively from its serial number. But there are ways to mitigate this uncomfortable situation.

1961–1969 Numbers

The dating chart presented in table E has been put together after consulting existing factory records. It is quite accurate for the period 1961–1966, which is not plagued by the steady duplications that began in 1967. It is nonetheless important to take into account the specifications of a model (and even check out its very existence during the period) before assessing the vintage of a 1960s Gibson. For example, there is no such thing as a 1967 Les Paul, whatever the serial number may seem to suggest.

Table F gives a few glorious examples of the duplications that occurred during the 1960s. Some six-digit numbers may also be occasionally followed by a letter (A, B, C, etc.) so as to cover several instruments of the same type issued at about the same time with the same serial number.

1970–1975 Numbers

The early 1970s instruments can be set apart thanks to a few discriminating features that did not exist earlier, such as a MADE IN USA stamp impressed below the serial number or volute on the back of the peghead.

However, within the period 1970–1975, there are regrettably no user-friendly records that permit useful groupings. In this respect table G is a reminder that:
• Almost any six-digit number can surface on guitars made during the 1970–1975 period;
• The various sequences were used pretty much at random.

TABLE F

DUPLICATION IN 1960S IMPRESSED NUMBERS
Selected items with actual registration dates

No.	Model	Ledger Date
140036	Firebird III	November 13, 1963
140036	ES-330TDC	November 17, 1967
330770	SG Std	August 18, 1965
330770	SJN	December 4, 1967
330770	ES-335TDC	January 8, 1968
400011	Melody Maker	December 20, 1965
400011	ES-330TD	February 7, 1966
400011	ES-335TD	November 29, 1967
400011	FT-45 (Cortez)	December 8, 1967
400011	B-45-12	January 3, 1968
500172	EB-0	October 18, 1965
500172	Melody Maker B.	July 8, 1968
500172	J-160E	August 2, 1968
500172	J-50	August 27, 1969
800089	J-45	May 2, 1966
800089	Melody Maker	July 27, 1966
800089	J-45	April 5, 1967
800089	ES-335TDC	May 1, 1967
800089	ES-335TD	February 1, 1968
800089	SJN	July 17, 1969
800089	ES-335TD	September 3, 1969
900605	SG Junior	December 19, 1966
900605	SG Custom	February 21, 1967
900605	B-25	February 22, 1968

Only the specifications and the availability of a model can help with an approximate dating of a 1970–1975 guitar during this period of major changes at Gibson.

In the course of 1973, possibly in an effort to help the factory customer service, a prefix letter was added on the six-digit numbers assigned to many acoustics (e.g., J-55 with #A400915). Then, in mid-1974, Gibson switched to B-prefixed numbers and gradually moved through the alphabet up to F-prefixed numbers, although E and F numbers are very rare. Beginning with letter C, these seven-digit numbers were also applied to electrics.

These seven-digit prefixed numbers were issued concurrently with standard six-digit numbers. For instance:

- ES-175D with #184481 and J-50 with #A600607 both issued on January 3, 1974

- L-6S with #394714 and Hummingbird with #B000005 both issued on December 13, 1974

The limited edition models released in the early '70s (e.g., Les Paul Custom with Alnico pickup) are normally stamped with LE plus a six-digit number while other reissues, like the 1971 Flying V and the 1972 Firebird V, have a medallion impressed into the body.

TABLE G

IMPRESSED HEADSTOCK NUMBERS 1970–1975
Basic chart with estimated series/years

Series	Year					
00000ls				. . . 1973		
100000s	1970	1971	1972	1973	1974	
200000s			1972	1973	1974	1975
300000s					1974	1975
400000s					1974	1975
500000s					1974	1975
600000s	1970	1971	1972		1974	1975
700000s	1970	1971	1972			
800000s	1970			1973	1974	1975
900000s	1970	1971	1972	1973		
Axxxxxx				1973	1974	1975
Bxxxxxx					1974	1975
Cxxxxxx						1975
Dxxxxxx						1975
Exxxxxx						1975
Fxxxxxx						1975

HEADSTOCK DECALS: 1975–1977

After a plethora of duplications, which probably made life difficult for the customer service department, Gibson suspended the six-digit numbers impressed into the headstock and replaced them in 1975 with an entirely new date-coded system.

Style and Location

The scheme introduced in 1975 consists of eight-digit numbers applied with a decal on the back of the peghead. This decal, in black or gold depending on the finish, also features the name of the model (not always correctly, though!) and the words "MADE IN U.S.A.," plus, if appropriate, the words "LIMITED EDITION."

More interestingly, the new number is date-coded via a two-digit prefix followed by six digits in the 100,000s and 200,000s to rank each instrument. This scheme lasted only from 1975 until 1977, and during this period the three prefixes used were:

- 99 for 1975
- 00 for 1976
- 06 for 1977

Comments on Usefulness

These 1975–1977 numbers are reliable for dating instruments as long as the decal on the peghead has not been tampered with.

IMPRESSED EIGHT-DIGIT NUMBERS: 1977–PRESENT

1977 saw the inception of an innovative scheme designed to overcome all the shortcomings of the previous numbers. This scheme was so well-conceived, it is still in operation, to everyone's satisfaction, 30 years after its introduction.

Style and Location

The eight-digit numbers premiered in August, 1977, follow a standard pattern reading YDDDYPPP in which:

- YY, i.e., the first and fifth digits show the year of issue
- DDD indicates the day of issue in the YY year
- PPP indicates the daily production ranking

In addition, numerical bands were created in PPP to indicate which Gibson plant built the instrument. At the outset the following bands were used:

- 001-499 was for Kalamazoo
- 500-999 was for Nashville (opened in 1974)

When Kalamazoo closed down in 1984, the lower band remained unused until 1989, when it was reallocated to the acoustics built in Bozeman, Montana. Subsequently, the band for Bozeman was brought down to 000-299 in 1990 while the Nashville band was enlarged to 300-899.

These eight-digit numbers are (deeply) impressed into the back of the peghead. On hollow bodies they are also mentioned on the paper label glued inside the body. The rectangular labels introduced on the threshold of the 1970s lasted barely a decade before white (and slightly later, also orange) old-style oval labels mentioning the serial number were again phased in.

Comments on Usefulness

The meaning of the eight-digit numbers does not require any dating chart. They are sufficient to log not only the year, but also a day of issue for every instrument, even though this is not the day it was finished and/or shipped from the factory. For instance:

- #80920017 belongs to a J-50
  made in 1980 (= 8---0---)
  on the 92nd day of that year (= -092----), i.e., on Tuesday, April 1, 1980
  in Kalamazoo (= ----017) where it was the 17th instrument on that day
- #91897355 belongs to a Les Paul Standard
  made in 1997 (= 9---7---)
  on the 189th day of that year (= -189----), i.e., on Tuesday, July 8, 1997
  in Nashville (= -----355) where it was the 55th instrument on that day

- #00476002 belongs to an SJ-200
  made in 2006 (= 0---6---)
  on the 47th day of that year (= -047----), i.e., on Thursday, February 16, 2006
  in Bozeman (= -----002) where it was the 2nd instrument on that day

There is, however, one major pitfall in the scheme in use since 1977. As of January 1994, the meaning of the eight-digit numbers on the Nashville-made instruments was (temporarily) changed to YYRRRRRR in which:

- YY indicates the year of issue
- RRRRRR is a cumulative ranking in the year

For instance:

- #94056358 belongs to an Explorer
  made in 1994 (= 94------)
  in Nashville where it ranked 56,358th in the year
  and NOT made on the 405th day of 1996(!)

Unlike Nashville, however, the Bozeman factory continued to use the regular format throughout 1994 on its acoustics. For instance:

- #93044025 belongs to a J-200 Ray Whitley
  made in 1994 (= 9---4---)
  on the 304th day of that year (= -304----), i.e., on Friday, October 31, 1994
  in Bozeman (= -----025) where it was the 26th instrument on that day
  and NOT made in 1993 as the 44,025th instrument in the year

The reason behind this Nashville oddity is unclear, but in any case the modified pattern lasted only one year and was phased out by January, 1995.

It is also worth noting that:

- The mandolins and dobros produced in Nashville since 1997 display another scheme reading YMMDDPPY in which:
  - YY – i.e., the last and the first digits indicate the year
  - MM indicates the month in the year
  - DD indicates the day of the month
  - PP indicates the daily ranking
- Some high-end archtops made in Nashville display numbers in the 000-299 brackets normally used for Bozeman-made acoustics. For instance:
  - Super 400CES #92345002 (1995)
  - L-5CESN #91216014 (1996)
  - L-5 Studio #90697014 (1997)
- July, 2005, saw the inception of nine-digit numbers featuring a YDDDYPPPP format with four digits instead of three for the production ranking, but an unchanged dating formula. So far these enlarged numbers seem to appear exclusively on Les Paul guitars. For instance:
  - Les Paul Studio Premium #034850654 (2005)
  - Les Paul Goddess #006261483 (2006)
  - Les Paul Standard #027670389 (2007)

OTHER SERIAL NUMBERS: 1979–PRESENT

Over the past three decades other types of serial numbers have been used in addition to the standard eight- (or nine-) digit format introduced in 1977.

Early 1980s Heritage and Custom Shop Models

Most of the Heritage Les Paul models produced between 1981 and 1983, like the Korina-bodied Flying V, Explorer, and Moderne, were released with special inked-on four-digit numbers consisting of a letter prefix (A, B, C, etc.) slightly apart, followed by three numerals. Similar numbers were also used at that time on early Custom Shop editions like the then-new Chet Atkins classic electrics.

1983–1992 Les Paul Reissues

In 1983 Gibson launched its first own attempt at re-creating a late 1950s Les Paul Standard, not to be confused with the contemporary Heritage 80 or the Standard 82. Initially made in Kalamazoo, and then in Nashville after Kalamazoo was shut down, these reissues feature an inked-on number of the same format (Y-xxxx) as the original 1950s instruments, with Y showing the last digit of the year of production. For example: #8-0592 comes on a 1988 instrument. This system can be found on the first-period Les Paul reissues until the beginning of 1993.

1990s and 2000s Les Paul Classics

The Les Paul Classic series, which debuted in 1990 as a modern rendition of the 1960 Les Paul Standard, is fitted with the same numbering scheme (Y-xxxx) as the 1980s reissues. The first of the five-digit inked-on numbers indicates the year of issue. For example:

- #1-3746 on a 1991 Les Paul Classic
- #4-3002 on a 1994 Les Paul Classic

Beginning in 2000, however, the number was enlarged from five to six digits with a YYxxxx format in which the last two digits of the year serve as a prefix. For example:

- #010358 on a 2001 Les Paul Classic
- #040504 on a 2004 Les Paul Classic

The inked-on digits used on this series are slightly bigger than those used on the vintage reissues.

1994 Centennial Models

Whereas the 12 models made in Bozeman come with standard eight-digit numbers (albeit with a specific label), the Centennial models made in Nashville feature a bespoke serial number embossed on their tailpiece. Each of the 12 Centennial models from Nashville was produced in runs of 101 pieces numbered from 1894 to 1994, with a one- or two-digit suffix indicating the month of release in 1994. For example: #1958-1 belongs to a Centennial Double Cutaway Les Paul Special (released in January, 1994).

Historic Collection: Les Paul Reissues

In 1992 Gibson launched a major program for the production of more faithful replicas of its vintage classics. These more accurate reissues have been grouped under the Historic Collection banner. Starting January 1, 1993, the new HC Les Paul reissues were introduced with a modified inked-on number reading M-Yxxx (not Y-xxxx as on the Les Paul Classic series) in which:

- M indicates the model code; and NOT THE YEAR OF ISSUE
- Y indicates the last digit of the year of manufacture

The main Historic Collection model codes used on Les Paul guitars since 1993 are:

- 9 for a '59 style LP Standard (e.g., 9-0052 from 2000)
- 8 for a plain-top 1958-style LP Standard (e.g., 8-3053 from 2003)
  or, for an LP Standard with a cherry-red top
  or, for a reissue of the 1958 Mary Ford model
  or, for an LP Jr. double cutaway (TV or cherry-red finish)
- 7 for a '57 style LP Custom with two or three humbuckers (e.g., 7-1879 from 2001)
  or, for an LP goldtop with two humbuckers
  or, for an LP Jr. with single cutaway
- 6 for a '56 style LP goldtop with P-90 pickups and TOM bridge (e.g., 6-5080 from 2005, but it could also be a 1995 number)
- 4 for a '54 style LP goldtop with a bar tailpiece (e.g., 4-3018 from 2003)
  or, for an LP Custom with Alnico pickup and P-90

- 2 for a '52 style LP goldtop with a trapeze tailpiece (e.g., 2-2004 from 2002)
- 0 for a '60 style LP Standard with slim neck and reflector knobs (e.g., 0-7189 from 1997, but it could also be a 2007 number)
  or, for a '50s style LP Special with single cutaway

As was already the case in the 1950s, the five-digit number (Y-xxxx) changes into a six-digit number (Yxxxxx) if, and when, required by production output. For example:

- #991851 on a '59 style LP Standard from (late) 1999
- #761173 on a '57 style LP Custom from (late) 2006

Also, since 2004, the HC Les Paul reissues made with a (lighter) chambered mahogany body—sometimes unofficially referred to as the Cloud 9 series—come with an inked-on number prefixed with CR and no space between the numerals. For instance: CR96016 on a '59 style LP Standard from 2006.

Great care should be exerted when sorting the pre-1993 Les Paul reissues and 1990s Les Paul Classics (all numbered with Y-xxxx) from the Historic Collection reissues (numbered with M-Yxxx). For instance:

- Les Paul Goldtop RI #9-0560 = 1989 (not 1990 or 2000)
- Les Paul HC 1959-style #9-3007 = 1993 (not 1989 or 1999)
- Les Paul Classic #6-0197 = 1996 (not 1990 or 2000)
- Les Paul HC 1956-style #6-0062 = 2000 (not 1996)

Distinguishing between a 1990s and a 2000s edition of the same Historic Collection model—e.g., between a 1996 and a 2006 LPR-9—cannot be done on the strength of the serial number alone. If the accompanying paperwork does not help, the easiest way is to check the codes on the potentiometers or the finer details of the reissue as Gibson has kept on improving the historic minutiae of the various reissues since 1993; witness the latest VOS features.

Finally, it should be noted that, contrary to the certificate of authenticity of the Fender Custom Shop, the certificates issued by Gibson do not carry a date of issue; presumably because the serial numbers of the HC models (or from the Gibson Custom Shop) are date-coded.

Modernistic Guitars HC Reissues

Various types of inked-on numbers can be found on the limited number of Futura, Flying V, and Explorer reissues produced since the early 1990s. In the mid-'90s, model codes were (temporarily) set as follows: 1957 Futura (7-Yxxx), 1958 Flying V (8-Yxxx), and 1959 Explorer V (9-Yxxx). For instance:

- #8-8099 on a 1998 Flying V reissue
- #9-8028 on a 1998 Explorer reissue

However, in the 1998 Historic Collection catalogue, the model designations were changed for 1958 Explorer and 1959 Flying V! Since the late '90s six-digit inked-on numbers like #991830 (1999) or #931307 (2003) have appeared on Flying Vs. At the same time, several Flying V reissues were built with Custom Shop numbers (see page 44).

Other Solid-Body HC Reissues

The reissues of classic solid-bodies from the 1960s like the SG or the reverse Firebird are usually fitted with an impressed number reading YYxxxM in which:

- YY indicates the last two digits of the year of issue
- M indicates the model code

As of this writing, the model codes commonly found on these 1960s reissues appear to be:

- 1 for the 1961-style SG Custom and Special (e.g., 970291 on 1997 LP/SG Custom reissue)
- 2 for the 1962-style SG Standard (with or without vibrato) (e.g., 060222 on a 2006 SG Standard)
- 3 for the 1963-style reverse Firebird I (e.g., 990443 on a 1999 Firebird)
- 4 for the 1964-style reverse Firebird III (e.g., 990424 on a 1999 Firebird III)

- 5 for the 1964-style reverse Firebird V or VII (e.g., 000065 on a 2000 Firebird VII)
- 8 for the 1968-style Les Paul reissues (e.g., 024288 on a 2002 LP Std goldtop)

The indication of the year with two digits (instead of one) removes the possibility of any confusion between a 1990s and a 2000s edition of the same model.

Thinline and Hollow Body HC Reissues

On the thinline and hollow body reissues the rationale is to replicate the A-series numbers from the 1950s, hence a format reading A-MYxxx in which:

- M indicates the model code
- Y indicates the last digit of the year

As of this edition, the principal model codes currently retained for these reissues are:

- 3 for the 1963-style ES-335TD with block markers (e.g., A-37003 on a 2007 ES-335)
- 4 for the 1964-style ES-330TD (e.g., A-49002 on a 1999 ES-330)
- 5 for the 1965-style ES-345TD (e.g., A-59015 on a 1995 ES-345)
- 9 for the 1959-style ES-335TD with dot inlays (e.g., A94009 on a 2004 ES-335)

The 1959-style ES-355 reissue also uses 9 as its model code, but its number comes with a specific B-prefix and reads B-9Yxxx. For example:

- #B-98095 on a 1998 ES-355TDN
- #B97034 on a 2007 ES-355TDC

Given that a single digit is used to indicate the year, the serial number alone is not sufficient to distinguish between a 1990s and a 2000s edition of the same model. As already mentioned, pot codes and/or any accompanying paperwork should be examined to log the correct year (even if the Gibson certificate of authenticity is not dated).

Custom Shop Instruments

In addition to the HC reissues, the Custom, Art, and Historic division of Gibson also makes various guitars based on vintage or recent designs. These instruments, which always feature a Custom Shop decal on the back of the headstock, do not necessarily carry a specific serial number, and they can be found with a regular eight-digit number of YDDDYPPP format.

Among those featuring a different number, the early CS instruments have an inked-on number of the same format as the LP Classic series (Y-xxxx). Later in the 1990s, the number was briefly changed to a YYxxxx format (e.g., #791178 on a 1997 ES-336) before the current CSYxxxx format with a CS prefix was activated. For example:

- #CS11675 on a 2001 Flying V
- #CS60595 on a 2006 LP Custom

Signature Models

The Signature models released by Gibson usually come up with a bespoke number when they are made by the Custom, Art, and Historic division. For instance:

The 2003 Gary Rossington SG models have a date-coded number almost similar in format to the 1960s reissues, but it is inked-on (not impressed) and reads 1-Yxxx.

The Johnny A models feature a JA xxx style number, which is not date-coded. The accompanying paperwork or the pot codes should be used for dating purposes.

The same holds true for the Jimmy Page limited edition from 2004 featuring PAGE xxx inked on the back of the headstock. The subsequent non-LE variant sports a JPP xxx style number also inked-on.

Depending on the period of issue, the dating of a Gibson guitar by its serial number may be fraught with difficulties. In some cases a few structural features, typical of Gibson instruments, may be of help determining the vintage of a guitar. The vagaries of 1960s and early 1970s numbers are notorious, and this is why this section will examine features likely to enable you to discriminate between instruments issued during that period. Of course, when attempting to date an instrument, it is advisable to check its specific appointments and their evolution in available reference books (see "Suggested Readings" at the end of this book).

MADE IN U.S.A. STAMP

Up to 1970 only the Gibson instruments made for export sometimes displayed a MADE IN THE U.S.A. mention, impressed in tiny letters near the edge of the headstock. Beginning in 1970, a much bolder mention was stamped into the wood on the rear headstock below the serial number. This second MADE IN U.S.A. stamp (Note: no "the" compared to the previous variant) is a useful discriminating feature to differentiate an early 1970s from a 1960s instrument.

HEADSTOCK VENEER

Up to 1970 the headstock veneer of Gibson guitars was made of white wood tinted in black, but it often proved prone to weather checking. In order to remedy this cosmetic shortcoming, a more stable black fiber head veneer was gradually introduced in 1970. Like the MADE IN U.S.A. stamp, it is a very useful feature for distinguishing between a late '60s instrument with a tinted white Holly veneer and an early '70s one built with a faultless black fiber head face.

If the type of material is not sufficiently clear at a glance, it is best to check the edge of the veneer in the truss rod routing on the headstock, and if absolutely necessary, to scratch the edge of the veneer gently. The original tinted Holly head face has since been brought back in the 1990s on the Historic Collection models.

HEADSTOCK PITCH

The headstock pitch is the sloping back angle of the headstock with the neck. The purpose of this angle is to allow the strings to press firmly against the nut because, as a rule, the deeper the angle, the better the string tension. Conversely, because of the straight grain construction of the neck and headstock, a deeper angle may result in damage should the instrument fall to the ground.

Up to 1965 Gibson guitars were built with a pitch set at a standard 17° angle. In late 1965 the pitch angle was slightly reduced to 14° in an attempt to make the headstock slightly stronger. This appointment may be helpful to distinguish the period of issue of a 1960s instrument in which the serial number is ambiguous. That said, it is very hard to spot a 17° versus a 14° pitch on a stand-alone basis, but the 3° difference is obvious when comparing side-by-side two instruments built with different headstock pitches.

After the advent of the volute on the back of the headstock (see below), Gibson felt it was possible to revert to a more pronounced headstock tilt. The 17° pitch first reappeared in 1973 on the revamped SG series, and both 14° and 17° variants remained in use during the 1970s and 1980s. The drive toward reproducing old-style features brought back the 17° pitch during the 1990s.

HEADSTOCK VOLUTE

In order to strengthen the headstock pitch, a volute—or reinforcement heel—first appeared on certain Gibson instruments on the threshold of 1970. At first this volute was fairly smooth, but it soon evolved into a prominent heel with a clear-cut ridge. Between 1970 and 1974, all Gibson guitars were gradually fitted with this appointment, the top-end archtop models being the last to follow suit.

Original "The Gibson" logo,
slanted on the headstock

Late 1920s "The Gibson" logo,
inlaid straight across the
headstock

Mid-1930s thin logo

Late 1930s thick logo

Mid-1940s thick logo, slanted on
the headstock

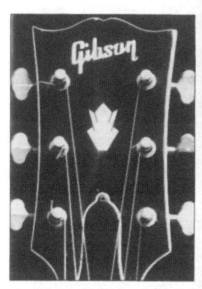

Late 1940s "Gibson" logo, with the
"i" dot visibly linked to the "G"

As previously mentioned, the advent of the volute enabled Gibson to reinstate the classic 17° headstock pitch on certain models like the SG series in 1973. Despite its structural merits, the headstock volute did not prove popular with players, and it was eventually phased out from all Gibson instruments by 1981. Today it is clearly perceived as a typical 1970s feature. Like the MADE IN U.S.A. stamp or the fiber headstock veneer, the volute can be useful to distinguish an early '70s from a 1960s instrument.

POT SOURCE CODE

The date coded source system described in the Fender section is also applicable in its principle to Gibson and may help in setting a hard floor (i.e., the earliest possible year of issue) for the dating of an instrument. On Gibson electrics, the most commonly-found codes and manufacturers are:

- 134: CentraLab
- 137: CTS Corporation
- 215: IRC (Note: code 615 in the late 1940s)

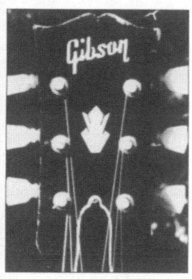

"Classic" post-war logo, with open "b" and "o"

Late 1960s pearl logo, without the dot of the "i"

Early "pentographed" logo, as used in the late 1960s

Early 1970s "pentographed" logo, without the dot of the "i"

Late 1970s thin logo

Post-1981 logo, with an upper link between "o" and "n"

It should be noted, however, that the electrics made since the mid-'90s do not always have pots coded with the standard industry format reading CCCYYWW. The newer pots may come with a distinct format reading MYCCCxxxxx in which:

- M shows the month code (1 to 9, then X-Y-Z for last quarter)
- Y shows the last digit of the year
- CCC is the manufacturer's code (usually 440 for CGE)
- xxxxx is the product reference

JUMBO FLAT-TOP FEATURES

From late 1968, Gibson's Jumbo flat-top acoustics went through a series of successive design changes. Some of these changes may be very useful for differentiating late '60s from early '70s instruments. Four evolutionary features are particularly of interest in this respect.

The Top/Bottom Belly Bridge Design

Until late 1968, most flat-top acoustics (except the J-200 and the Dove) were fitted with a top-belly bridge, i.e., a bridge where the carved ridge was designed to withstand the strings' pull points toward the soundhole. The top-belly bridge design was originally introduced in late 1949 on models like the Southern Jumbo and the J-45/50, before being successively fitted to the J-185, the J-160E, the Hummingbird, and the Everly Brothers.

After late 1968 Gibson switched over to a bottom belly bridge, i.e., a bridge in which the ridge faces the lower bout and supports the strings' pins. For the record, the bottom belly was Gibson's first enlarged bridge design, as used on the 1940s Southern Jumbos. The bottom belly bridge remained in production until 1983 when the acoustic line underwent another major design overhaul.

The Bolted Bridge

From the mid-'30s until the late '60s Gibson used a pair of bolts, as well as glue, to hold the bridge on most flat-tops. A bolted bridge can be identified by the decorative pearl dots covering the bolt heads. The bolts can also be seen by inserting a dentist's mirror inside the body under the bridge area. However, when an original Gibson bridge has been repaired, it is not unusual to find that the bolts have been removed.

The earliest bottom-belly bridges from the late '60s can be found with a bolted bridge. In 1969, however, Gibson dropped the bolts and relied exclusively on glues to hold the bridge in place. This structural change also prompted the withdrawal of the two decorative pearl dots.

The Adjustable Bridge Saddle

The adjustable bridge saddle first appeared in 1955 as a standard feature on the then-new J-160E, and as an option on selected models. By 1960 it became a regular appointment on mid-range flat-tops, while top-end models like the J-200 and the Dove were equipped with a Tune-O-Matic bridge. In 1971 the adjustable saddle was removed and replaced by a stationary one when Gibson introduced a much flatter bridge design. The final samples with an adjustable saddle are usually found on models with a glued-on (i.e., no bolts) bottom-belly bridge.

The Double-X Bracing Pattern

A fairly standard X-bracing pattern with varying features was used by Gibson on its better flat-tops until the early 1970s. In 1971, a double-X bracing design was introduced to make the guitars more robust and less subject to warranty work. This design is characterized by a second X glued within the lower quadrant of the main X braces in lieu of the classic tone bars. The double-X pattern is not visible from the outside, and one needs a dentist's mirror to see it under the top. However, it is a typical feature of the flat-tops built between 1971 and 1984. As such it is another useful feature to distinguish early '70s from late '60s instruments. Also, the flat-tops with a double-X bracing logically feature a glued-on (i.e., no bolts) bottom-belly bridge without any adjustable saddle.

GIBSON HEADSTOCK LOGO

The earliest guitars produced by the Gibson Mandolin-Guitar Mfg. Co. do not usually feature any brand name on the headstock, but rather a crescent and/or a star (like Orville's instruments) or nothing at all. From 1908, however, most Gibson instruments began to display "The Gibson" in the form of a slanted pearl inlay placed on the upper end of the peghead. This remained the standard trim until the late 1920s. By the late 1920s, "The Gibson" gradually ceased to be slanted on certain models and was inlaid straight across the peghead. On the earliest flat-tops (L-O and L-1) the slanted script was not inlaid in pearl but silk-screened in silver.

The period from 1928 to 1934 saw a gradual withdrawal of "The Gibson" in favor of just "Gibson." The upper-end models were fitted with a pearl script while the lower-end models sported a brand name silk-screened in white. The mid-1930s saw the introduction of a thicker pearl script on upper-end models like the new Super 400, and by the end of the decade most instruments were fitted with what is commonly called the thick pre-war logo inlaid straight across the peghead.

When production resumed after WWII, the same old script was briefly retained, albeit in a slanted position on the headstock. However, the acquisition of Gibson by Chicago Musical Instruments (C.M.I.) in 1944 prompted the advent of a new corporate trademark, which quickly found its way on the guitars. Beginning in late 1947 the so-called modern logo gradually began to appear on all the instruments, inlaid in pearl on the upper-end models and silk-screened in gold on lower-end models. The late 1940s design is still the basic ornament of Gibson guitars more than 50 years after its inception, but a few subtle variations in design may be distinguished over the years.

The earliest pearl variant used between 1947 and 1951 is characterized by its open, or broken, "B" and "O" while the "i" dot is visibly connected to the "G." These features are not found on the silk-screened versions, which have an unbroken "b" and "o." By the end of 1951 the "i" dot ceased to be visibly connected to the capital "G," but the broken "b" and "o" remained typical of the logo until the late 1960s.

In late 1967, a Gibson logo made with a pentograph (i.e., not cut, but outlined with black finish) debuted. The early pentographed units are more square-sided and feature a closed "b" and "o." However, because pearl-cut logos were held in stock, the pentographed logos did not appear on production models until mid- to late 1968, while old-style pearl-cut logos can be found until 1969. Both variants overlapped, but the pentographed unit is typical of 1970s instruments. In the course of 1968 another engineering change brought about the removal of the dot on the "i." Consequently, both traditional and pentographed logos can be found without the dot on the "i" at the end of the 1960s.

The inception of a black-fiber head veneer in the course of 1970 brought about a slightly smaller variant, characterized by thinner lettering and small bulges in the "s," and as before, a closed "b" and "o."

From 1972 the dot on the "i" reappeared on some instruments but, according to factory records, it was not until late 1976 that it was officially reinstated with a slightly increased diameter. Third-party supplies already in stock probably explain why both types may be found during the 1970s.

In 1981 the design was marginally modified to feature an upper link between "o" and "n," as opposed to a lower link on the original late 1940s variant.

Before the 1980s Gibson had begun to understand the value of certain details thanks to the requirements of a few dealers and collectors. The Les Paul Standard reissues specially made for vintage dealers in the late 1970s were the first instruments to feature original style pearl-cut logos.

The change of ownership in 1986 prompted a greater attention to detail and brought about a sense of compromise between old-style features and modern, more consistent production methods. The Gibson logo is no exception, and recent models, both electric and acoustic, display the modern logo as originally designed in the 1940s with its typical broken "b" and "o" and a lower link between "o" and "n."

1917 Special Grand concert guitar, Style "O." The first Gibson with a cutaway body.

1962 Super 400CESN with a pointed Florentine cutaway

Les Paul Standard, the "Dream Guitar" of many players

1962 Les Paul/SG Standard with vibrato tailpiece set into a pearl inlaid ebony block

1964 Firebird VII in Custom color; a rare combination

1960 ES-335 TDN with "dot inlay" fretboard, P.A.F. pickups, and long pickguard

Short-scale ES-350T from 1958

One-off L-5 from 1935, custom-built with a round soundhole instead of the traditional twin *f*-holes

Custom-built J-185 electric from 1963

1959 Flying V. One of Gibson's most radical and innovation designs.

1962 Double 12 (or EDS 1275). One of the last double necks made with a hollow body and a spruce top before Gibson changed for an SG style body.

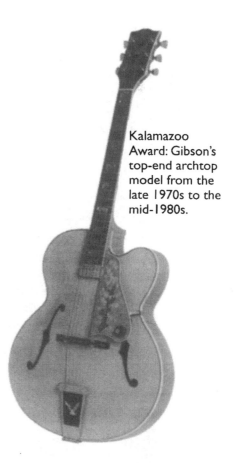

Kalamazoo Award: Gibson's top-end archtop model from the late 1970s to the mid-1980s.

The Fred Gretsch Mfg. Co. was founded by Friedrich Gretsch (1856–1895), a German immigrant who, in 1883, set up shop in Brooklyn, New York, for the production of drums, tambourines, and banjos. By the turn of the century, Gretsch was one of the leading importers and manufacturers of musical merchandise. The earliest Gretsch-branded guitars appeared in late 1933 and began to rival Gibson and Epiphone in the field of archtop orchestra models.

By all accounts, Gretsch reached its guitar zenith during the 1950s and 1960s thanks to a string of innovative designs by Jimmie Webster, not to mention the company's long association with legendary guitarist Chet Atkins. Gretsch is also widely acknowledged today as the first to have used colorful automotive finishes on several of its regular models. After 1967, however, various changes in ownership and management gradually led to a loss of creativity, and the popularity of the models marketed during the 1970s began to wane.

Although the company stopped producing guitars in the United States in early 1981, some instruments were reportedly assembled until 1983. In 1985 the great-grandson of the founder acquired the Gretsch brand name, and he turned to a Japanese manufacturer to restart production of Gretsch guitars. In 1989 Fred Gretsch Enterprises Ltd., headquartered in Savannah, Georgia, began marketing modern replicas of some of the great classics of the past. Since January, 2003, the Fender Musical Instruments Company has been in charge of the marketing and distribution of Gretsch guitars worldwide.

FOREWORD ON GRETSCH NUMBERS

The dating of Gretsch guitars has long seemed a puzzling exercise. This was partly due to the shortage of information until the 1990s, and partly because Gretsch had ceased all production when the brand enjoyed a wave of post-Beatles popularity in the 1980s. Indeed the 1984 edition of *Guitar Identification* was the first book with enough detailed information to assess the vintage of Gretsch instruments! Since then other publications have helped re-establish Gretsch's credentials in the guitar pantheon.

Three basic numbering schemes have been used on Gretsch guitars since their inception in the mid-'30s, but on the whole they are not inscrutable, even if they cannot be checked against old factory ledgers. In fact, it remains to be seen whether some of the original company records still exist, or if they have disappeared forever, possibly in the two fires that damaged the plant in Booneville, Arkansas, in 1973.

The serial numbers used after late 1965 are date-coded and pose no real challenge in assessing the vintage of a Gretsch instrument. Their varying format from three to six digits used to be a source of confusion, but this should no longer be the case.

In the same way automobile manufacturers slightly alter their new models each year, Gretsch minutely modified the specifications of its models each year. And although the changes seem confusing at first, valuable information can be gleaned from them. Minute details can make the difference and allow for a reasonably accurate dating chart for pre-1966 Gretsch instruments. Even so, it is a good idea to look for unusual appointments that may surface on a Gretsch when attempting to assess its vintage!

THE ORIGINAL SERIES: 1939–1965

Between the late 1930s and the mid-'60s Gretsch actually used only one single consecutive numbering scheme on its guitars, beginning with three-digit numbers running from 001 up to five-digit numbers ending in the 84,000s.

Style and Location

These 84,000+ numbers were applied in a number of ways through the years, and it is of prime importance to check HOW and WHERE they show up on a guitar, particularly since many of them could be confused with the post-1965 date-coded serial numbers.

In the late '30s Gretsch began penciling a three-digit number on the inside back of its higher-end archtop models. Lower-end instruments from the '40s do not feature any number at all and can only be dated by their specifications and key structural features.

After WWII, when normal production resumed, serial numbers were also impressed onto the top edge of the headstock regardless of the status of the model. During the late '40s both body-penciled numbers and head-impressed numbers may be found on Grestch instruments, but as already mentioned, they all belong to the same consecutive scheme.

Beginning in 1949, serial numbers were first stamped on a paper label glued inside the body. In addition to the serial number (usually in red ink), this label also features the reference number of the model in the catalogue rubber-stamped in black or dark blue ink. Penciled numbers were then phased out, but on certain instruments numbers continued to be impressed in the headstock up to the very early 1950s.

TABLE A
ORIGINAL SERIES 1939–1965

Year	Estimated Series
Pre-1950	001s/1000s/2000s
1950	3000s
1951	4000s/5000s
1952	5000s/6000s
1953	6000s/7000s/8000s
1954	9000s
	10,000s/11,000s/12,000s
1955	12,000s/13,000s/14,000s
	15,000s/16,000s/17,000s
1956	17,000s/18,000s/19,000s
	20,000s/21,000s
1957	22,000s/23,000s/24,000s
	25,000s/26,000s
1958	26,000s/27,000s/28,000s/29,000s
	30,000s
1959	30,000s/31,000s/32,000s/33,000s/34,000s
1960	34,000s
	35,000s/36,000s/37,000s/38,000s/39,000s
1961	39,000s
	40,000s/41,000s/42,000s/43,000s/44,000s
	45,000s
1962	45,000s/46,000s/47,000s/48,000s/49,000s
	50,000s/51,000s/52,000s/53,000s
1963	53,000s/54,000s
	55,000s/56,000s/57,000s/58,000s/59,000s
	60,000s/61,000s/62,000s/63,000s
1964	63,000s/64,000s
	65,000s/66,000s/67,000s/68,000s/69,000s
	70,000s/71,000s/72,000s/73,000s/74,000s
	75,000s/76,000s/77,000s
1965	77,000s/78,000s/79,000s
	80,000s/81,000s/82,000s/83,000s/84,000s

The paper label issued between 1949 and 1957 is commonly referred to as the "white" Fred Gretsch label. It features the original name and the address of the company, i.e., THE FRED GRETSCH MFG. CO. - 60 BROADWAY BROOKLYN 11, N.Y.

On hollow bodies the label is found on the inside back beneath the upper f-hole of archtops or beneath the single soundhole of flat-tops. On the (so-called) solid-bodies such as the Duo-Jet introduced in 1954, it is glued either in the controls cavity or on the underside of the main plastic back plate. In this case, however, the number is not visible from the outside. This is why it is also normally "scratched" onto the outside of one of the plastic back plates, usually the smaller one over the switches' cavity.

1957 saw the advent of a slightly modified label that remained in use until 1965. It is characterized by a grey top-end and an orange background for the words "THE FRED GRETSCH MFG. CO." On this second variant, which appeared about #25,000, the serial number is pre-printed in slightly smaller black numerals, while the model number is ink-stamped with dark ink.

In addition to the orange Fred Gretsch label, serial numbers belonging to the original series also materialized simultaneously in three other ways during the period 1958–1965.

On models like the Duo Jet and the Jet Fire Bird, the serial numbers continued to be simultaneously "scratched" onto one of the back plates. Indeed, some early 1960s instruments may be found with simply this scratched-on number and no paper label glued on the underside of the main back plate.

Mid-'50s serial number (09319) stamped on a white Fred Gretsch label. Note the model number (6014-5) referring to a Synchromatic 100 archtop guitar.

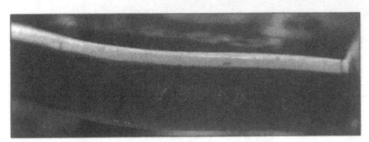

The tiny numerals of a mid-'60s number (76656) impressed on the top edge of the headstock of a Chet Atkins 6120 with Electrotone body

Serial number (12115) "scratched" onto the back plate of a mid-'50s 6130 Round Up

This serial number is also stamped on the white Fred Gretsch label located in the controls cavity of the same instrument.

Beginning in 1958, top-end models (like the White Falcon and the Country Gentleman) were often fitted with a serial number etched on the metal name plate affixed on the headstock.

The inception of the Electrotone hollow bodies in 1962 (see page 63, "Electrotone Body") prompted Gretsch to resurrect numbers impressed on the top edge of the headstock of certain models such as the 6120 Chet Atkins Hollow Body and the Chet Atkins Tennessean. This method was also used on the true solid-bodies introduced in the early '60s like the Corvette.

Comments on Usefulness

Notwithstanding their distinct styles and locations, all the serial numbers used between 1939 and 1965 belong to the same consecutive series. Based upon the detailed specifications of the guitars issued during this period, a dating chart can be formulated for easy reference.

Despite the absence of support documentation from company records, the chart shown in table A should, with a one-year tolerance, allow for the dating of all instruments. It is recommended, however, to always check the appointments of a Gretsch guitar, especially any unusual ones, to corroborate the dating derived from this chart.

DATE-CODED SERIAL NUMBERS: 1965–1972

In late 1965 the original series was replaced by a new scheme in which new-style date-coded numbers were impressed on the back of the headstock. In the process paper labels mentioning the serial number were phased out.

Style and Location

The 1965–1972 date-coded numbers are tinted in white, gold, or black according to the guitar's finish. The location of the numbers on the back of the headstock, along with their tinted color and larger size makes it impossible to confuse them with the previous impressed numbers. Additionally, in the wake of the Baldwin takeover announced in May, 1967, the words "MADE IN U.S.A." were added ahead of the serial number in late 1967.

Early '60s number (46383) printed on the Fred Gretsch label with orange top introduced in 1957. This label belongs to a 6129 Silver Jet and is glued on the underside of the controls back plate.

May, 1976, serial number (5-6xxx) penciled on a black and white Gretsch Guitars label

97: September, 1969, number (99xxx) with the words MADE IN U.S.A. introduced in late 1967

96: December, 1966, number (126xxx) impressed into the back of the headstock

The basic format of the 1965–1972 numbers is either MYxxx or MMYxxx in which:

- M or MM shows the month of production in the year (1 to 12)
- Y indicates the last digit of the year of production (e.g., 5=1965)
- xxx indicates the progressive count of guitars in that month

It should be noted, though, that xxx does not necessarily imply that three numerals are always mentioned after the digit for the year. Experience shows that this serialization scheme produced numbers featuring between three (i.e., MYx) and six (i.e., MMYxxx) digits. Sometimes there is a small space between the first digit and the rest of the number, but it does not affect the dating formula.

Comments on Usefulness

The five and six-digit numbers are usually no problem to decipher, provided that five-digit numbers are not confused with those in the original series described previously.

For example: #67683 actually belongs to a June 1967 Country Gentleman, but there is actually a Gretsch instrument from 1964 carrying #67683 under the prior numbering scheme. In such instances the style and location of the serial number (and of course the availability of the model during the period) are critical factors to determine the correct date of issue.

Some of the five-digit numbers commencing with 10, 11, and 12 could also be interpreted in two ways. For example: #12619 actually belongs to a December 1966 Tennessean (126xx) and not to a January 1972 Tennessean (12xxx). In this instance, the absence of the "MADE IN U.S.A." imprint ahead of the number rules out the possibility that it could be a 1972 instrument.

For instruments made between late 1967 and 1972 and carrying a five-digit number beginning with 10, 11, or 12, only the structural features (e.g., the type of truss rod adjuster), the specific appointments of the model, or its very existence during this period can help in determining the correct vintage. Likewise the three- and four-digit numbers may also create confusion. They are theoretically coded MYx, MYxx, or MMYx, yet rare exceptions patterned after Yxx and Yxxx should not be totally ruled out. Also, replacement necks intended for repair were allegedly impressed with just xxx.

To illustrate further this user-friendly scheme for dating Gretsch guitars, table B shows selected examples with their codes explained. Date-coded numbers impressed on the back of the headstock were phased out in late 1972 after the production of Gretsch guitars was moved to the Booneville facility in Arkansas.

DATE-CODED SERIAL NUMBERS: 1973–1981

At the end of 1972, numbers impressed on the back of the headstock were discontinued and Gretsch reverted to paper labels for identification purposes.

Style and Location

The third-style rectangular label is white with a solid black frame, looking a bit like a funeral invitation heralding what would be the demise of Gretsch guitars a decade later! The label reads simply "GRETSCH GUITARS" with a small "MADE IN U.S.A." at the bottom, without any indication of the company's (changing) address.

The 1973–1981 black labels mention the serial number as well as the model reference number penciled in black. The latter was revamped in 1972 with a "7" prefix instead of a "6" prefix. As was the case before, the new-style label is either glued on the inside back of hollow bodies (with true f-holes reinstated in 1972) or inside the controls cavity.

Comments on Usefulness

Regardless of the change of style and location of the numbers, the date-coded scheme adopted in 1965 remained in effect. After 1972, however, the numbers on black labels frequently feature a hyphen between the first digit(s) showing the month and the digit indicating the year. This hyphen eliminates the potential risk of confusion identified with the 1967/72 numbers commencing with 10, 11, or 12. Moreover, the count of guitars in the month consistently features three digits including zeros in the first and second positions if appropriate.

TABLE B

NUMBERS IMPRESSED ON HEADSTOCK 1965–1972

Selected items with date coding
M and MM = month (1 to 12); Y = last digit of the year

Model	Serial Number		Dating
Viking	105312	MMYxxx	October 1965
Tennessean	8683	MYxx	August 1966
Corvette	96372	MYxxx	September 1966
Monkees	126999	MMYxxx	December 1966
12-String Electric	1791	MYxx	January 1967
Black Hawk	57232	MYxxx	May 1967
Rally	107312	MMYxxx	October 1967
Rancher	787	MYx	July 1968
Van EPS 7-String	6890	MYxx	June 1968
White Falcon	68763	MYxxx	June 1968
Country Gentleman	118159	MMYxxx	November 1968
Duo Jet	3995	MYxx	March 1969
New Yorker	19953	MYxxx	January 1969
Country Gentleman	99110	MYxxx	September 1969
Tennessean	3037	MYxx	March 1970
Nashville	70252	MYxxx	July 1970
White Falcon	110327	MMYxxx	November 1970
Viking	3167	MYxx	March 1971
Viking	41066	MYxxx	April 1971
Super Chet	121057	MMYxxx	December 1971
12-String Electric	8252	MYxx	August 1972
Viking	72084	MYxxx	July 1972
Super Chet	102261	MMYxxx	October 1972

TABLE C

NUMBERS ON PAPER LABELS 1973–1981

Selected items with date coding
M and MM = month (1 to 12); Y = last digit of the year

Model	Serial Number		Dating
Country Gentleman	1-3848	M-Yxxx	January 1973
Broadkaster	8-4175	M-Yxxx	August 1974
Double Anniversary	9-4121	M-Yxxx	September 1974
Country ROC	1-5065	M-Yxxx	January 1975
Van EPS 7-String	10-5156	MM-Yxxx	October 1975
White Falcon	6-6156	M-Yxxx	June 1976
Tennessean	10-6060	MM-Yxxx	October 1976
Nashville	3-7082	M-Yxxx	March 1977
Super Axe	11-7145	MM-Yxxx	November 1977
Ccommittee	5-8180	M-Yxxx	May 1978
TK-300	12-8328	MM-Yxxx	December 1978
Roc Jet	1-9039	M-Yxxx	January 1979
BST-5000	12-9023	MM-Yxxx	December 1979
Country Gentleman	2-0082	M-Yxxx	February 1980
White Falcon	11-0315	MM-Yxxx	November 1980

Bearing in mind the above, the basic format of the date-coded numbers issued between 1973 and 1981 is either M-Yxxx or MM-Yxxx with all three x positions duly completed. To illustrate this second scheme of date-coded numbers, a few selected examples have been gathered in Table C with their dating explained. This was the final scheme applied to Gretsch guitars made in the U.S.A. before the production was stopped in early 1981, almost a century after the foundation of the Fred Gretsch Company.

TRANSITIONAL NUMBERS: 1970–1973

In mid-1970 the production of Grestch guitars was relocated from Brooklyn, New York, to Booneville, Arkansas, where Baldwin, the new owner, already had manufacturing facilities. Perhaps as a direct consequence of this transfer and the disruption it caused, a different type of serial number can be found occasionally on some instruments made in the early 1970s.

Style and Location

These rare early 1970s transitional numbers are all made up of five digits in the 10,000s or in the 20,000s. They do not incorporate any date coding, and judging from the few examples known to this author, they appear to follow a consecutive pattern. For example: #10024 on a Double Anniversary or #26055 on a Tennessean.

On the last electrics made with the closed Electrotone body, these five-digit numbers can be found impressed on the top edge of the headstock, albeit with taller digits than those used in the late 1940s or in the early 1960s. In most cases, though, they are printed (not stamped) in black on a paper label displaying a grey top-end and orange background, and reading "THE FRED GRETSCH MFG. CO." (like the 1957–65 labels) but with the unusual mention "THAT GREAT GRETSCH SOUND" at the bottom.

Reproduction of the card issued in late 1957 to explain the Neo-Classic Fingerboard story

Reproduction of the original Gretsch OK card for a 6120 Nashville Western issued in August, 2006 (0608xxxx)

Comments on Usefulness

After checking some of these five-digit numbers with the available records of Gretsch distributors in Europe, it would appear that the company temporarily used drum labels and numbers on its guitars.

Based on the specifications of some 1970s instruments displaying such five-digit numbers, it would appear that these unusual labels and numbers were used until at least 1973, thereby fuelling the theory that they also came in as substitutes when the Booneville plant was damaged by two fires in 1973. In other words, there could well have been two waves of five-digit transitional numbers: a first one in 1970 when the guitar plant was moved to Arkansas and a second one in 1973 when the plant twice caught fire.

CONTEMPORARY NUMBERS: 1989–Present

The Japanese-made Gretsch guitars marketed since late 1989 are all fitted with date-coded serial numbers, which are quite easy to decipher despite having more numerals. Two successive schemes can be found depending on the year of issue:

1. The number on the guitars marketed between 1989 and 2002 have a basic format reading YYMmmm(m)-x(xx) or YYMMmmm(m)-x(xx) in which:

- YY indicates the last two digits of the year (e.g., 89 = 1989)
- M or MM indicates the month in the year (1 to 12)
- mmm(m) indicates the model reference number with three or four digits albeit without the 6 or 7 prefix (e.g., 6120 reads 120)
- the final x(xx) refers to a one- to three-digit production count

For instance:

- a Country Classic I (model 6122-S) #9111122S-120 can be dated to November, 1991 (9111)
- a Sparkle Jet (model 6129) #965129-768 can be dated to May, 1996 (965)
- a Nashville (model 6120) #01720-2719 can be dated to July, 2001 (017)

2. The number on the guitars marketed since 2003 feature a two-letter prefix (JD, JT, or JF) followed by a standard eight-digit number reading YYMMxxxx in which:

- YY indicates the last two digits of the year (e.g., 05 = 2005)
- MM indicates the month in the year (01 to 12)
- xxxx refers to a production count

For instance:

- an Anniversary (model 6118) #JT03010067 can be dated to January, 2003 (0301)
- a Black Falcon (model 6136) #JT05118329 can be dated to November, 2005 (0511)
- a Chet Atkins Country Gentleman (model 6122) #JT07082815 can be dated to August, 2007 (0708)

HELPFUL DATING FEATURES

Certain features typical of Gretsch guitars may be of assistance in assessing the vintage of a given instrument, particularly if it does not have a date-coded serial number. Gretsch guru Jay Scott believes that the company was so rigid and fastidious on its features and models' appointments that they can be used alone to date instruments with accuracy.

This section will modestly consider a limited number of generic Gretsch features while suggesting that, if necessary, the specific appointments of each model be checked in available dedicated publications (see the "Suggested Reading" at the end of this book).

MODEL PX CODES

Gretsch instruments usually have both a namesake (e.g., the Chet Atkins Hollow Body) and a reference number or PX code (e.g., model 6120). While the name is sometimes written explicitly on the headstock or on the pickguard, only the model code is indicated on the label (if any) showing the serial number. It may be useful to identify a model correctly before attempting to assess its vintage. This is why the main PX codes used on guitars between 1949 and 1981 have been listed in a chart with their corresponding model designations (see page 62).

A Few Pointers for the Lay Reader

Between 1949 and 1971 Gretsch models were identified by four-digit numbers beginning with 6 (i.e., PX6xxx). After 1971 Baldwin introduced fresh reference numbers prefixed with 7. Later in the 1970s the Beast series came out with 8xxx product codes, but the other models were discontinued with 7xxx codes in the early 1980s. A given PX code refers not only to a model, but also stipulates its finish if several options are available. For example: the mid-'60s Viking may be referred to by three distinct codes because it was offered in three finishes, i.e., PX6187 in Sunburst, PX6188 in Natural, and PX6189 in Cadillac Green.

On some early '50s instruments the label shows a dual product code, e.g., 6014-5, 6190-1, or 6192-3 regardless of the finish. In a few cases the same code was applied to different models over the years. For example, this happened with PX6189, which originally referred to the Streamliner in the 1950s before being applied to the Cadillac Green Viking in the mid-1960s.

Conversely the same name was sometimes used on entirely different instruments with distinct product codes. For example: the Streamliner designation was first applied to a 16-inch archtop hollow body in the 1950s (PX6189-90-91) before resurfacing on a thin-body electric in the late 1960s (PX6102-03).

HEADSTOCK LOGO

Two main variants can be found on Gretsch guitars.

1. Most of the instruments from the 1930s and 1940s feature what is commonly referred to as the old Gretsch script, placed in a slanted position on the headstock. In the early 1950s it was recut in a straighter position across the headstock on models like the Electromatic, the Electro II, or the Duo Jet. The generalization of the T-roof logo after 1953 led to the discontinuation of the old-style script, which may be found until about 1958 on high-end archtops such as the Eldorado and the Fleetwood.

2. The T-roof logo with block lettering—in which the top T-bar extends from G to H—first appeared in the 1930s as a corporate feature before being applied with a shorter T-bar on a few flat-tops. In the late 1940s it was fitted to the 6050 New Yorker archtop and the 6007 Sierra flat-top, and later on the 6002-03 flat-tops, albeit in a slanted position on the headstock. On these models the logo is engraved in a two-ply plastic head veneer with a white bottom ply.

In 1954 the T-roof logo became the standard appointment, except on models such as the Eldorado/Fleetwood high-end archtops (which often retained the old-style script logo until about 1958) and the White Falcon and its sibling the White Penguin (both fitted with a vertical block-letter logo until 1958). By 1959 all the Gretsch guitars were branded with the T-roof logo, positioned straight across the headstock, except on models like the archtop New Yorker and Corsair, where it can be found in a slanted position. This remained unchanged until production stopped in 1981. Only late 1970s models like the TK-300 or the infamous Beast series feature slightly different Gretsch logos amidst many un-Gretsch appointments.

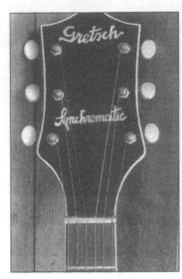

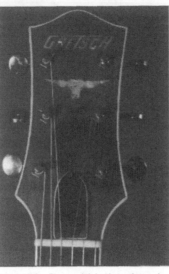

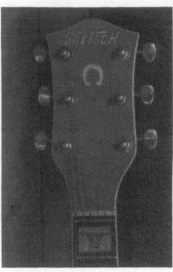

Early 1950s Synchromatic headstock with the old-style Gretsch script. Note the absence of the truss rod cover above the nut.

Mid-'50s Round Up headstock with T-roof logo. Note the small bullet-shaped truss cover above the nut.

Early 1960s Jet Fire Bird headstock. Note the enlarged truss rod cover compared to the one fitted to the Mid-'50s Round Up.

The enlarged headstock of a 1970s Roc Jet. Note the absence of a truss rod cover above the nut due to the Burns Gearbox.

ZERO FRET

In 1959 Gretsch introduced a zero fret on all the Chet Atkins models, thereby obviating the need for the metal nut requested by the Nashville picker. Commonly found on European guitars, the zero fret was turned into the "adjustable rod-actionflo neck" in Gretsch brochures. By 1960 the zero fret was consistently installed on top-end models like the White Falcon, the Country Club, and the Sal Salvador. By 1962 it was also fitted on the double cutaway Jet series, and then on most of the new models marketed during the 1960s like the Viking, Astro-Jet, Monkees, and Van Eps.

NEO-CLASSIC FINGERBOARD

Among the many features that instantly set a Gretsch guitar apart, few are more easily spotted than the half-moon (or thumbprint) inlays of the Neo-Classic Fingerboard. The concept first appeared in 1957, slightly before the inception of the Filter'Tron pickup, as suggested by the various transitional instruments combining DeArmond pickups and half-moon inlays.

- The Neo-Classic Fingerboard was initially fitted to all the better models in the Gretsch catalogue, while dot-inlays were kept on the New Yorker, Clipper, Rambler, and subsequently on the Corvette, Bikini, Princess, and the basses.

- At the outset an ebony fretboard was an integral part of the Neo-Classic concept, but mid-range models soon switched to a less expensive rosewood one like the Anniversary models in 1960 and the Tennessean in 1962. In the late '60s rosewood was also used instead of ebony on the Country Gentleman and the Nashville, while the Jet models often came out with an "ebonized" fingerboard.

- The Ronnie Lee and the Monkees Rock 'n' Roll models have double Neo-Classic inlays as a standard feature, that is, half-moons inlaid on each side of the fretboard. This appointment can also be found occasionally on some Nashville and Tennessean guitars as well as on some left-handed instruments.

- In 1964 Gretsch premiered its T-Zone Tempered Treble on the White Falcon and Viking models, identified by its offset dot inlays from the 15th to the 21st fret. Later, the Blackhawk, Rally, Sam Goody, and Streamliner introduced in 1967 all shared the same hybrid fretboard featuring half-moons (1st to 12th frets) and dot-inlays (15th to 19th frets).

Unlike many other classic Gretsch features, the Neo-Classic fingerboard escaped the early 1970s Baldwin overhaul and can be found on the better models until production stopped in 1981. In 1974, though, the White Falcon single and double cutaway models went back to block inlays.

Old-style script

T-roof logo

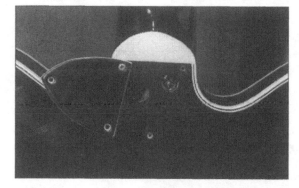

The metal nameplate (without serial number) of a Chet Atkins Nashville

The Burns Gearbox located in the neck heel is typical of the Gretsch instruments made after 1970.

This close-up of a mid-1960s Nashville shows the fake *f*-holes of the Electrotone body, the standby switch placed near the rim, the single muffler with its flip lever switch, and the B1 Bigsby vibrato tailpiece with the typical V cutout.

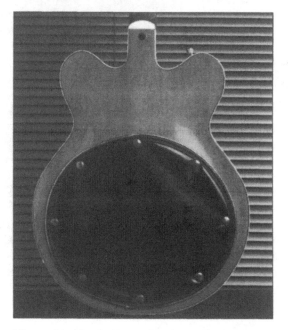

The padded back. Also note the dark plug in the upper part of the back meant to conceal the heel dowel.

METAL NAME PLATE

Metal plates engraved with the name of the model first appeared in 1958 on the headstock of the Anniversary models, the Country Gentleman, and the White Falcon. Subsequently other models—such as the White Penguin (1959), Ronnie Lee (1962), Viking (1964), Chet Atkins Tennessean (1965), Monkees (1966), Chet Atkins Nashville (1966), Blackhawk (1967), Streamliner (1967), Sam Goody (1967), Van Eps (1968), and Roc Jet (1969)—were fitted with it.

For the record, the solid-body Astro-Jet introduced in 1963 also displayed a metal nameplate, but it was fixed on the body and not on the headstock. This typical Gretsch appointment was discontinued with the move to the Booneville plant, and it is not found on post-1970 instruments.

POST-WAR GRETSCH MODEL DESIGNATIONS

6xxx numbers (1949–1971)

6000 Golden Classic Hauser model
6001 Silver Classic Hauser model
6002 Burl Ives Junior flat-top
    then Folk (sunburst)
6003 Grand Concert flat-top
    then Jimmie Rogers Singing
    then Folk Singing
    then Folk
6004 Burl Ives flat-top
    then Folk (mahogany)
6005 Ozark (nylon strings)
6006 Electro Classic
6007 Synchromatic Sierra flat-top
6008 Wayfarer Jumbo flat-top
6009 Jumbo flat-top (sunburst)
6010 Sun Valley flat-top
6014 Synchromatic 100 H/B (sunburst)
    then Corsair H/B (sunburst)
6015 Synchromatic 100 H/B (natural)
    then Corsair H/B (natural)
6016 Corsair H/B (Bordeaux Burgundy)
6020 12-string flat-top
6021 Synchromatic 125F flat-top
    then Town and Country flat-top
6022 Rancher
6023 Bikini guitar
6024 Bikini bass
6025 Bikini double neck
6028 Synchromatic 160 (sunburst)
6029 Synchromatic 160 (natural)
6030 Synchromatic 100 with cutaway (sunburst)
    then Constellation (sunburst)
    then Sho-Bro Spanish
6031 Synchromatic 100 with cutaway (natural)
    then Constellation (natural)
    then Sho-Bro Hawaiian
6036 Synchromatic 300 (sunburst)
6037 Synchromatic 300 (natural)
6038 Synchromatic 300 with cutaway (sunburst)
    then Fleetwood (sunburst)
    then Eldorado with 17-in. body (sunburst)
6039 Synchromatic 300 with cutaway (natural)
    then Fleetwood (natural)
    then Eldorado with 17-in. body (natural)
6040 Synchromatic 400 (sunburst)
    then Eldorado with 18-in. body (sunburst)
6041 Synchromatic 400 (natural)
    then Eldorado with 18-in. body (natural)
6042 Synchromatic 400F flat-top
6050 New Yorker H/B
6070 Electric Bass (long scale/1 PU)
6071 Electric Bass (short scale/1 PU)

6072 Electric Bass (long scale/2 PU)
6073 Electric Bass (short scale/2 PU)
6075 12-string Electric (sunburst)
6076 12-string Electric (natural)
6079 Van Eps 7-string (sunburst)
6080 Van Eps 7-string (walnut)
6081 Van Eps 6-string (sunburst)
6082 Van Eps 6-string (walnut)
6100 Black Hawk (sunburst)
6101 P.O.S. Country Club (sunburst)
    then Black Hawk (Jet Black)
6102 P.O.S. Country Club (natural)
    then Streamliner (sunburst)
6103 P.O.S. Country Club (Cadillac Green)
    then Streamliner (Cherry Red)
6104 Rally (Rally Green)
6105 Rally (Bamboo Yellow/Copper Mist)
6106 Princess (all finish)
6109 Twist
6110 Twist (w/vibrato tailpiece)
6111 P.O.S. Anniversary (sunburst)
6112 P.O.S. Anniversary (two-tone Smoke Green)
6115 Rambler ¾ scale
6117 Double Anniversary (sunburst) also mid-'60s
    electrics with cat's eyes soundholes
6118 Double Anniversary (2-tone Smoke Green)
    also mid-'60s Anniversary with two-tone
    tan finish
6119 Chet Atkins Tennessean
6120 Chet Atkins Hollow Body
    then Chet Atkins Nashville
6121 Chet Atkins Solid-Body
6122 Chet Atkins Country Gentleman
6123 Monkees Rock'n'Roll model
6124 Anniversary (sunburst)
6125 Anniversary (two-tone Smoke Green)
    also mid-'60s Anniversary with two-tone
    tan finish
6126 Duo Jet 4-string baritone uke
    then Astro-Jet
6127 Duo Jet 4-string tenor guitar
    then Roc Jet (Porsche Pumpkin)
6128 Duo Jet
6129 Silver Jet
6130 Round-Up
    then Roc Jet (Mercedes Black)
6131 Jet Fire Bird
6132 Corvette S/B with one pickup (mahogany)
    then Corvette S/B with one pickup (red)
6133 Corvette S/B with one pickup (Platinum Grey)
6134 White Penguin
    then Corvette S/B with one pickup +
    vibrato (red)

6135 P.O.S. Penguin
    then Corvette S/B with two pickups + vibrato
6136 White Falcon (mono)
6137 White Flacon (stereo)
6182 Corvette H/B (sunburst)
6183 Corvette H/B (natural)
6184 Corvette H/B (Jaguar Tan)
6185 Electromatic H/B
6186 Electromatic Spanish Guitar outfit (with amp)
    then Clipper (sunburst)
6187 Electro II H/B (sunburst)
    then Clipper (Lotus Ivory/Metallic Grey)
    then Viking (sunburst)
6188 Electro II H/B (natural)
    then Clipper (natural)
    then Viking (natural)
6189 Electromatic H/B (2 PU)
    then Streamliner (Bamboo Yellow/Copper Mist)
    then Viking (Cadillac Green)
6190 Electromatic H/B (sunburst)
    then Streamliner (sunburst)
6191 Electromatic H/B (natural)
    then Streamliner (natural)
6192 Electro II with cutaway (sunburst)
    then Country Club (sunburst)
6193 Electro II with cutaway (natural)
    then Country Club (natural)
6196 Country Club (Cadillac Green)
6199 Convertible
    then Sal Salvador

7xxx numbers (1971–1981)

7495 Electro-Classic
7505 Folk (sunburst)
7506 Folk (natural)
7514 Sun Valley (sunburst)
7515 Sun Valley (natural)
7525 Rancher
7535 Deluxe flat-top
7545 Supreme flat-top
7555 Clipper
7560 Double Anniversary (sunburst)
7565 Streamliner (sunburst)
7566 Streamliner (Cherry Red)
7575 Country Club (sunburst)
7576 Country Club (natural)
7577 Country Club (antique maple)
7580 Van Eps 7-string (sunburst)
7581 Van Eps 7-string (walnut)
7585 Viking (sunburst)
7586 Viking (natural)
7593 White Falcon (single cutaway)
7594 White Falcon (double cutaway)

7595 White Falcon-Stereo (double cutaway)
7600 Broadkaster S/B (natural)
7601 Broadkaster S/B (sunburst)
7603 Broadkaster H/B with vibrato tailpiece (natural)
7604 Broadkaster H/B with vibrato tailpiece (sunburst)
7605 Broadkaster bass S/B (natural)
7606 Broadkaster bass S/B (sunburst)
7607 Broadkaster H/B (natural)
7608 Broadkaster H/B (sunburst)
7609 Broaskaster H/B w/Terminator tailpiece (Red
    Rosewood)
7610 Roc Jet (Black)
7611 Roc Jet (Porsche Pumpkin)
    then Roc Jet (Jet Black)
7612 Roc Jet (Cherry Red)
7613 Roc Jet (walnut)
7615 Electric Bass S/B
7620 Country Roc
7621 Roc II
7623 Corvette S/B with two pickups
7624 TK-300 (Autumn Red)
7625 TK-300 (natural)
7626 TK-300 bass (Autumn Red)
7627 TK-300 bass (natural)
7628 Committee
7629 Committee bass
7632 Deluxe Corvette
7655 Chet Atkins Tennessean
7660 Chet Atkins Nashville
7670 Chet Atkins Country Gentleman
7676 Country Squire
7680 Deluxe Chet (Autumn Red)
    then Super Axe (red)
7681 Deluxe Chet (walnut)
    then Super Axe (ebony)
7682 Super Axe (sunburst)
7685 Atkins Axe (ebony)
7686 Atkins Axe (Rosewood Red)
7690 Super Chet (Autumn Red)
7691 Super Chet (walnut)
7705 Sho-Bro Hawaiian 6-string
7710 Sho-Bro Hawaiian 7-string
7715 Sho-Bro Spanish

8xxx numbers (1979–1981)

8210 BST-1000 1PU (mahogany)
8211 BST-1000 2PU (red)
8215 BST-1000 2PU (mahogany)
8216 BST-1000 1PU (red)
8217 BST-1500 with two DiMarzio pickups (mahogany)
8220 BST-2000 (mahogany)
8221 BST-2000 (red)
8250 BST-5000 (walnut/maple)

TRUSS ROD ADJUSTMENT

- The early Gretsch guitars have a laminated neck reinforced by a non-adjustable square rod embedded under the fretboard. It was not until the early 1950s that Gretsch introduced its first adjustable truss rod, accessible at the body-end of the neck through a small recess in the fretboard binding. This explains why, up to 1954, Gretsch guitars did not have a truss rod cover on the headstock.

- A conventional (Gibson-like) truss rod, adjustable above the nut, appeared in 1954. Except on the White Falcon and Penguin, the early variant is characterized by its small bullet-shaped cover, which was replaced in 1956 by an enlarged cover. The truss rod adjustable above the nut was fitted to most Gretsch instruments and remained a basic feature until 1970.

A few pre-1970 models, however, were equipped at times with a neck rod adjustable at the body-end of the neck. These exceptions are solid-bodies like the 1961–62 Corvette and Bikini or the 1962/63 Corvette-style Twist model.

- After 1970 the conventional Gretsch truss rod was replaced by the Burns Gearbox, named after the British guitar maker who designed it (and who had been acquired by Baldwin in late 1965). The Burns system is characterized by an adjusting bolt located on the back of the body next to the neck heel. It is easily identified by its triangular plastic cover. Cosmetically, like the pre-1954 guitars, the 1970s instruments are thus characterized by the lack of a truss rod cover on the headstock.

Of course, there are often exceptions to a Gretsch rule. For example, the Broadkaster hollow body was built with a conventional truss rod. In fact, this author has come across a thin-bodied Broadkaster featuring both a Burns Gearbox and a truss rod!

NECK HEEL DOWEL

In 1958 Gretsch began to use a heel dowel on most models in order to strengthen the neck-to-body junction. This involved inserting a wood screw in the neck heel and then concealing it with a circular cap made of dark wood. Depending on the models, the dowel cap shows either on the back of the body, directly on the heel, or in the cutaway.

The original heel dowel was abandoned in 1970 with the inception of the Burns Gearbox. However, the need for reinforcement remained, and the 1970s instruments have a screw securing the neck-to-body junction that is next to the truss rod adjusting bolt under the triangular Gearbox cover.

ELECTROTONE BODY

The following features are not decisive for dating a Gretsch instrument, but they may nonetheless provide a few useful cutoff points to determine a period of issue.

- One of Gretsch's best-known innovations was the inception in 1957 of the Chet Atkins Country Gentleman with a closed 17-inch body and fake f-holes. On the first single cutaway variant the simulated f-holes are usually made of inlaid black plastic, sometimes enhanced with a white border. Subsequently, f-holes were painted-on as production expanded. (Note: a few Country Gentlemen from 1959–1961 can be found with real—not fake—f-holes.)

- At the end of 1961 the closed body of the Country Gentleman led to what Gretsch called the Electrotone body premiered in 1962, i.e., a slimmer 1 7/8-inch thick variant with a double or a single cutaway. The Electrotone body with painted-on f-holes can be found on the Country Gentleman, Chet Atkins Hollow Body (later renamed Nashville), Chet Atkins Tennessean, and the two basses shaped after the Country Gentleman (long-scale bass) and the Tennessean (short-scale bass). The short-lived Ronnie Lee model was also fitted with the Electrotone body.

- The Electrotone body with fake f-holes was phased out shortly after the move to the Booneville factory. By 1972 all the Chet Atkins models reverted to real f-holes, albeit much smaller in size than the original design from the 1950s and 1960s.

PADDED BACK

The padded back is often associated with the Electrotone body because it was also premiered in 1962, and possibly because it may be perceived as a smart trick to conceal the opening cut in the Electrotone body to install the electronics.

Although it is a specific appointment of the 6120 and 6122 models made after 1961, the padded back is also found on guitars with real f-holes like the White Falcon, Country Club (in 1962 and 1963 only), Viking (introduced in 1964), and the late '60s 12-string electric built with a 17-inch body. The two Electrotone-bodied basses, as well as the Princess solid-body, were also fitted with a "padded back cushioned for comfort."

The Baldwin-inspired redesign that took place in 1971 did away with many original Gretsch features like the padded back, which survived only on the top-end White Falcon. By 1975 the padded back was definitively removed from both the double and single cutaway variants of the White Falcon.

MUFFLERS

Built-in bridge mutes, or mufflers as Gretsch called them, are another typical feature ushered in at the end of 1961. They came in either as a single muffler meant for the six strings, or on high-end models, as a double muffler consisting of two smaller pads enabling the player to mute either the three bass strings and/or the three treble ones. The early mufflers from 1962 are activated by one (single unit) or two (double unit) rotary control(s) fitted with a regular Gretsch knob. By 1963 the rotary controls were replaced by flip lever switches.

The Chet Atkins Hollow Body, the thin-bodied Country Club, the Viking, the two Electrotone-bodied basses, and the 12-string electric with a 17-inch body were fitted with a single muffler. The White Falcon and the Country Gentleman came out in 1962 with a double muffler. In 1964 the Country Club dropped its single muffler shortly before returning to a thicker 2 3/4-inch body, and by 1968 the Country Gentleman was downgraded to a single muffler.

Like several other Gretsch gizmos, mufflers did not survive the early 1970s Baldwin-inspired redesign except on the White Falcon, which was the only 7-series model to retain its double mufflers. The respite was short-lived, however, and by 1974 the mufflers were also removed on the White Falcon.

ELECTRICS' CIRCUITRY

Without listing all the setups found on Gretsch electrics, a few pointers can be useful for dating pre-1965 instruments without a date-coded serial number.

- Most of the two-pickup electrics made before 1954 are characterized by their "3+1" circuitry without any selector switch. The three knobs, set in triangular fashion near the treble f-hole, consist of two individual volumes for each pickup and one master control for mixing the two pickups. The "+1" is a master volume control located in the upper bout near the front pickup.

- The year 1954 saw the inception of a three-position selector switch, which was added on the upper bout opposite the master volume control. The previous mix control was changed into a real master tone control. The two-pickup electrics made between 1954 and 1957 are thus characterized by their "3+1" circuitry augmented by a pickup selector switch.

- The introduction of the Filter'Tron pickup in late 1957 brought in further changes. By 1958 the 3+1 circuitry gave way to a "2+1" layout as the master tone control was replaced by a three-position tone switch located next to the pickup selector switch.

Lay readers should beware of confusing the arrangement found on certain 1962 instruments with the 3+1 circuitry of the 1954–57 electrics. The confusion may be caused by the rotary dial-up control used in 1962 for the single muffler on models like the Chet Atkins Hollow Body and the Country Club. These 1962 models can be identified by the two switches (pickup and tone) located on the upper bout and/or by the red felt found under the muffler's knob.

Incidentally, a tone switch was also installed on single pickup electrics like the PX6119 Tennessean and the PX6125 Anniversary, which display only one volume knob. However, single pickup models like the hollow body Streamliner, Corvette, and Clipper retained a traditional circuitry with rotary volume and tone controls.

In 1958 Gretsch announced its Project-O-Sonic (P.O.S.) stereo circuitry initially characterized by:
* a three-position cut-off switch in lieu of a master volume control on the cutaway;
* Filter'Tron pickups with only one half of the poles exposed—under the bass strings on the neck pickup and the treble strings on the bridge pickup;
* a bridge pickup placed farther away from the bridge and closer to the neck pickup.

This first variant found on the PX6137 White Falcon and the Country Club in P.O.S. guise did not prove popular. Another stereo outfit was therefore introduced in late 1959 on the White Falcon, and slightly later on the Country Club. The second variant is characterized by four switches on the upper bout, i.e., three tone switches and one pickup selector switch. It also uses Filter'Tron pickups with all 12 poles exposed. Beginning in 1965, the four switches formerly placed on the upper bout were redistributed around the body lower rim of the PX6137 White Falcon, while the P.O.S. stereo wiring ceased to be available on the Country Club.

On the threshold of 1962 Gretsch completed its classic circuitry with a standby switch acting as an on/off switch for electrics so that they could be temporarily turned off without losing the tone settings. Placed near the jack output and the individual volume controls, the standby switch is found on most models with the notable exception of the Sal Salvador, Anniversary, Clipper, and Corvette. Unlike other Gretsch gizmos, the standby switch survived the Baldwin redesign and found its way onto several 7-series models until late 1978.

In the mid-'60s Gretsch produced a limited run of a guitar commonly known as the Cat's Eye Custom because of the shape of its soundholes. Apparently no official designation was ever coined for this electric, whose paper label (if any) portrays it as model 6117, although it shows no resemblance to a sunburst Double Anniversary.

In any case, this maverick, first made in 1964, is interesting because it was the first Gretsch electric ever to be fitted with a "4+0" Gibson-style circuitry. Each pickup has individual volume and tone controls, while pickup selection is operated via a three-way switch located on the round cutaway. Oddly for a 1960s Gretsch, this (rare) model did not feature a master volume control, a tone switch, or a standby switch.

In 1967 the new Gretsch Rally was introduced with a treble booster activated via a knob located next to the individual volume controls alongside the body rim. A similar treble booster was also added to the Duo Jet, Jet Fire Bird, and Corvette solid-body until these models were discontinued.

The Roc Jet introduced in late 1969 brought in a new "4+1" circuitry. A master volume was added to the individual volume and tone controls à la Gibson, while the three-position pickup switch was repositioned on the upper bout. As many classic Gretsch features were phased out in the early '70s, the 4+1 arrangement became the norm on the new Deluxe Chet, Country Club, and thin-bodied Broadkaster.

POT SOURCE CODE

The date-coded source system described in the chapter on Fender is also applicable to most Gretsch electrics and may help in setting a hard floor for the dating of an instrument.

1969 left handed Country Gentleman in an unusual (for the model) Cadillac Green finish

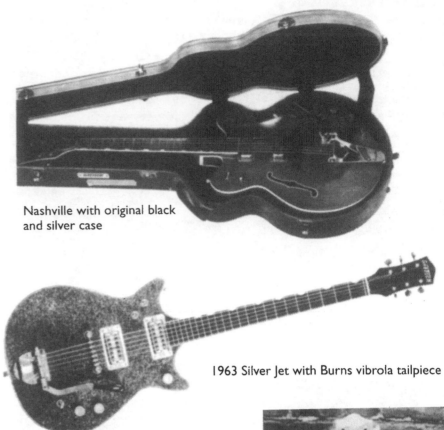

Nashville with original black and silver case

1963 Silver Jet with Burns vibrola tailpiece

1955 White Falcon featuring a vertical "Gretsch" logo on the headstock, engraved "humped" inlays on the fretboard, DeArmond pickups, Melita bridge, and "Cadillac" G tailpiece

1967 Corvette with asymmetric headstock and Burns vibrola

Mid-1950s Convertible, with suspended DeArmond pickup and controls mounted on the pickguard. This model was used as a basis for the late 1950s Sal Salvador.

1955 Round Up, with matching amplifier . . .wild wild West!

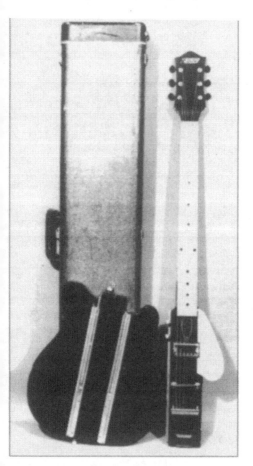

1961 Bikini with folding neck and special oblong case

Early 1950 Syncromatic "100"

1956 Chet Atkins hollow body (6120), featuring all the Western paraphernalia, namely "G" brand on the body, western motives on the fingerboard, longhorn inlay on the headstock, and "Chet Atkins" signpost logo on the pickguard

1959 Country Club, featuring the "Stereo Project-O-Sonic" wiring circuit

1968 Monkees Rock 'n' Roll model with double Neo-Classic inlays on the fingerboard

Guitar Identification 67

The C.F. Martin Company was established in 1833 in New York by Christian Frederick Martin (1796–1873) after he emigrated from Saxony. In 1839 he moved his business and family from New York to Nazareth, Pennsylvania, which is the birthplace of Martin guitars. Martin is indeed one of the oldest family-owned and operated music businesses in the world, and its current chairman, C.F. Martin IV, is the sixth generation of Martin descendants to run the company.

During the 1850s C.F. Martin perfected the famous X-bracing system for flat-top acoustics, as opposed to the prevailing fan and ladder bracings then found on contemporary instruments. The inception of Martin's X-bracing was a defining moment in the history of the American guitar. Another major Martin innovation was the Dreadnought body shape, originally commissioned by the Ditson Company in 1916 and widely imitated ever since.

Apart from less successful attempts in the field of archtop acoustics and later electrics, Martin guitars have ranked for decades among the finest flat-top guitars ever produced. New designs such as the M-series (1977) and the J-series (1981) have been developed in recent years to supplement the great classics of the pre-war era that continue to be the backbone of the Martin catalogue. Lavish and expensive prestige models like the D-50 Deluxe (in 2001) and the D-100 (in 2004), have been produced as limited editions to highlight the superlative craftsmanship of Martin instruments.

FOREWORD ON MARTIN NUMBERS

Unlike the three other American manufacturers dealt with in this book, Martin has been using the same numbering scheme for more than 100 years. And it works perfectly well for logging the exact year of issue of any guitar made since 1898. The year 2004 saw the production of the Martin guitar carrying #1,000,000.

Martin is well-known for keeping fairly detailed records of its production and, for those with access to these records, any 20th century instrument can be dated with total accuracy.

Only the pre-1898 instruments, often referred to collectively as "New York Martins," do not feature a serial number. Consequently their vintage can only be assessed on the strength of their specific appointments, a job that is often the preserve of true Martin specialists. A few features typical of 19th-century Martin guitars can help to elucidate the approximate period of issue of a guitar, unless there is a much welcome date penciled on the underside of the top as is sometimes the case!

Owing to the specificity of Martin guitars, the space dedicated to their serial numbers is obviously not as large as in the other chapters of this book.

SERIAL NUMBERS: 1898–PRESENT

A few years after succeeding his father in 1888, Frank Henry Martin, the founder's grandson, became interested in making mandolins. By 1895 the first mandolins were built, and for the first time in the company history, a serial number was used and applied on each of them. The inception of serial numbers on mandolins, combined with the end of a distributorship agreement, probably explains why guitars were finally numbered in 1898.

Style and Location

Beginning in 1898, a serial number was stamped on the neck block inside the body of all guitars, and sometimes also on the top edge of the headstock until about 1902. On the archtop models briefly produced during the 1930s and early 1940s, the number is usually stamped on the center backstrip.

The serialization scheme started from #8000, which was then retained as an estimate of the quantity of guitars produced since 1833. From then on Martin serial numbers progressed consecutively, i.e., the lower the number, the older the instrument. Thus #10,000 was assigned in 1905, #50,000 in 1932, #100,000 in 1947, #500,000 in 1990 and more recently, #750,000 in 2000 and #1,000,000 in 2004, which says a lot about the significant increase in recent production output after the Nazareth plant extension.

In October, 1930, the model designation (see below) was added above the serial number on the neck block. In 1984 Martin started using paper labels on certain limited edition models in order to display the signature(s) of the CEO, the model designation, sometimes with the ranking in the LE, the year of issue, and more recently the serial number.

The only guitars that do not follow the scheme inaugurated in 1898 are the 18 and 28 series solid-body electrics marketed between 1979 and 1983. These unusual (and ultimately unsuccessful) models for Martin were assigned a bespoke series beginning with #1000 and progressing on a consecutive basis.

In addition to their standard number, limited editions and signature models built in limited runs usually carry a "second" serial number on the paper label glued inside the body.

Comments on Usefulness

Thanks to consistent and diligent bookkeeping, the Martin ledgers allow precise dating of any instrument carrying a serial number. Only instruments made by employees for their personal use usually do not show any serial number, and they may prove hard to assess unless they feature a date penciled on the underside of the soundboard.

Moreover, the Martin company has never shown the kind of reluctance (or complete lack of interest!) of its American counterparts to address the vintage of its instruments. The company freely shares information and constantly updates the dating chart it has released for years, whether on its business card or more recently on its Web site. The dating chart featured in this book shows the first and the last number used each year since 1898. Bravo!

HELPFUL DATING FEATURES

Owing to the accuracy and consistency of the serialization scheme used since 1898, it is not essential to scrutinize post-1898 features to support or to crosscheck the dating of an instrument. For identification purposes, however, it may be useful to have a few pointers on Martin semantics that have not changed a great deal since the 1850s.

Assessing the vintage of pre-1898 Martin guitars is a real challenge, as they do not carry any serial number, or even any indication of the type of the model. During the 19th century (and 30 years into the 20th century), the paper label on the case was actually the only place showing the model designation. Dating "New York Martins" calls for a first-hand, superior knowledge of old Martins, even if a few features can be of use to the layman in determining at least the decade of issue.

MODEL DESIGNATION

Martin guitars are famous for their two-part designation meant to indicate first the body size as a prefix, and then, after a hyphen, the style or grade as a suffix. For example: 0-28 or D-45.

Numeric designations were first assigned in the early 1850s in an effort to standardize guitar shapes and their decorative style. The origin of the very first style numbers was apparently their wholesale price, while Gibson would later use the retail price to christen some of its models like the Super-400 or the J-200.

Up to 1930 the model designation was not mentioned anywhere on guitars; it could only be found on the case label (if at all). In October, 1930, the designation was (at last!) added on the neck block above the serial number. The guitars built by the Martin Custom Shop facility, formally inaugurated in March, 1979, may simply show "CUSTOM" on the neck block rather than a tentative conventional designation. Recent limited editions usually show their year of issue explicitly on the neck block.

Body Size

Numerals or letters are used to indicate the body size, e.g., 1, 7, 0, 00, D, M, J, B.

All the instruments with a similar letter or prefix theoretically share the same dimensions regardless of their style. However, this is not invariably correct as, for instance, the 12-fret neck and the 14-fret neck variants of D-size guitars do not have exactly the same measurements. In the modern post-war era, such differences normally attract a suffix for identification purposes, e.g., S on the old-style 12-fret D models.

The main prefixes used by Martin in relation to its model designations and sizes have been gathered in a chart for an easier consultation.

MARTIN SERIAL NUMBERS 1898–2007

Year	1st Number	2nd Number	Year	1st Number	2nd Number	Year	1st Number	2nd Number
1898	8000	8348	1935	58680	61947	1972	294271	313302
1899	8349	8716	1936	61948	65176	1973	313303	333873
1900	8717	9128	1937	65177	68865	1974	333874	353387
1901	9129	9310	1938	68866	71866	1975	353388	371828
1902	9311	9528	1939	71867	74061	1976	371829	388800
1903	9529	9810	1940	74062	76734	1977	388801	399625
1904	9811	9988	1941	76735	80013	1978	399626	407800
1905	9989	10120	1942	80014	83107	1979	407801	419900
1906	10121	10329	1943	83108	86724	1980	419901	430300
1907	10330	10727	1944	86725	90149	1981	430301	436474
1908	10728	10883	1945	90150	93623	1982	436475	439627
1909	10884	11018	1946	93624	98158	1983	439628	446101
1910	11019	11203	1947	98159	103468	1984	446102	453300
1911	11204	11413	1948	103469	108269	1985	453301	460575
1912	11414	11565	1949	108270	112961	1986	460576	468175
1913	11566	11821	1950	112962	117961	1987	468176	476216
1914	11822	12047	1951	117962	122799	1988	476217	483952
1915	12048	12209	1952	122800	128436	1989	483953	493279
1916	12210	12390	1953	128437	134501	1990	493280	503309
1917	12391	12988	1954	134502	141345	1991	503310	512487
1918	12989	13450	1955	141436	147328	1992	512488	522655
1919	13451	14512	1956	147329	153225	1993	522656	535223
1920	14513	15848	1957	153226	159061	1994	535224	551696
1921	15849	16758	1958	159062	165576	1995	551697	570434
1922	16759	17839	1959	165577	171047	1996	570435	592930
1923	17840	19891	1960	171048	175689	1997	592931	624799
1924	19892	22008	1961	175690	181297	1998	624800	668796
1925	22009	24116	1962	181298	187384	1999	668797	724077
1926	24117	28689	1963	187385	193327	2000	724078	780500
1927	28690	34435	1964	193328	199626	2001	780501	845644
1928	34436	37568	1965	199627	207030	2002	845645	916759
1929	37569	40843	1966	207031	217215	2003	916760	978706
1930	40844	45317	1967	217216	230095	2004	978707	1042558
1931	45318	49589	1968	230096	241925	2005	1042559	1115862
1932	49590	52590	1969	241926	256003	2006	1115863	1197799
1933	52591	55084	1970	256004	271633	2007	1197800	1268091
1934	55085	58679	1971	271634	294270	2008	1268092	

Decorative Styles

Numbers are used after the hyphen to indicate the style or grade, e.g., 18, 21, 28, 35, 38, 40, 45.

All the instruments with a similar number theoretically share the same decorative style, regardless of their body size, at least if they have been issued within the same period of time. In fact, the ingredients of the longest-serving styles, like 18 and 28, have not remained completely stable since their inception in the 1850s and 1860s. For instance, style 18 originally featured a body with rosewood back and sides before switching to mahogany in 1917.

The original rationale also held that the higher the number, the more lavish (and expensive) the wood and the decoration of the guitar. For example: style 45 offers fancier appointments than style 28. The modern era has somewhat dented this logic. The Bicentennial D-76 introduced in 1975 was not fancier (or more expensive) than a contemporary D-45, although it did cost more than a D-41.

A few years later, the maple-bodied guitars introduced in the mid-1980s were assigned 60-series styles, although they were not necessarily fancier than 40-series models. In fact, certain styles may be de facto restricted to specific body sizes. For instance, styles 60 and 62 are found only on Dreadnought guitars, styles 64 and 65 on M-sized, and style 65 on Jumbo-sized guitars. The same goes for style 35 introduced in 1965 and found almost exclusively on Dreadnought guitars.

It would take a complete book (Mike Longworth's and also Walter Carter's!) to list precisely the many combinations and changing attributes of Martin styles since the 1850s. Some of them date from the 19th century and may be quite difficult to expound. As a starting point, this book features a chart listing the styles in numerical order with their practical lifespan.

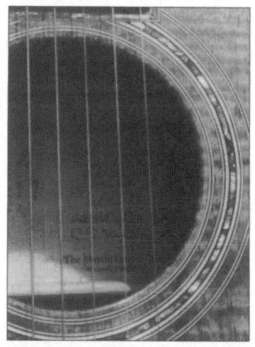

Paper label with serial number (604649) glued inside the body of a 1997 custom-built 000-45

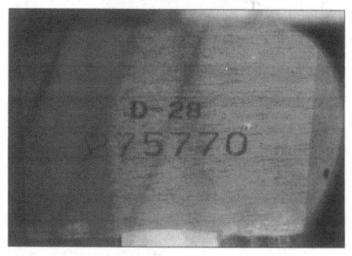

Serial number stamped on the neck block of a D-28 from 1971

Ad Hoc Suffixes

Another chart explains the main suffixes that have surfaced since 1917 to complete the model designations. For instance, H as in 00-18H is meant to indicate a guitar set for Hawaiian playing with a high nut, a high and non-slanted bridge saddle, and a flat fingerboard often with ground frets.

Few suffixes were actually used during the pre-war period (e.g., G for Gut strings, H for Hawaiian, K for Koa, P for Plectrum, T for Tenor). Most of the suffixes shown in the chart are of fairly recent origin as Martin enlarged its range of variants available for a given model while reproducing pre-war hallowed appointments. A suffix is also used to distinguish the signature models introduced since the mid-1990s. The tremendous success of the Eric Clapton 000-42EC from 1995 has prompted Martin to market a growing number of signature and commemorative models. For instance:

- Gene Autry's D-45GA
- Merle Haggard's 000C-28SMH
- John Mayer's OMJM
- Clarence White's D-28CWB

As of press time, close to a hundred signature models have been released by Martin, usually in the form of a limited run, as a tribute to artists both alive and deceased. The most successful among all the signature models is undoubtedly the Eric Clapton 000-28EC, which to date has been produced well in excess of 10,000 units.

BODY SIZE AND OTHER PREFIXES IN MODEL DESIGNATIONS

0   Concert body size with 13.50-inch width at lower bout and 24.9-in scale, e.g., 0-21. First listed in 1854.

00   Grand concert body size with 14 1/8-inch width at lower bout (14 5/16-inch on 14-fret neck guitars) and 24.9-inch scale, e.g., 00-18. First listed in 1873.

000   Auditorium body size with 15-inch width at lower bout and 24.9-inch scale (some with 25.4-inch), e.g., 000-42. First listed in 1902.

0000   Grand auditorium body size with 16-inch width at lower bout and 25.4-inch scale (identical to M-series), e.g., 0000-28. First listed in 1997.

1   Standard body size with 12.75-inch width at lower bout and 24.9-inch scale, e.g., 1-21. Listed from 1852 until the 1930s.

2   Ladies' body size with 12-inch width at lower bout and a 24.5-inch or a 24 3/8-inch scale, e.g., 2-17. Listed from 1852 until the 1930s.

2½   Ladies' body size with 11 5/8-inch width at lower bout and 24.5-inch scale, e.g., 2½-18. Listed from 1852 until the 1920s.

3   Small body size with 11 1/4-inch width at lower bout and 23 7/8-inch scale, e.g., 3-17. Listed from 1852 until the 1900s.

3½   Terz model body size with 10 11/16-inch width at lower bout and 22-inch scale. Listed from 1852 until the early 1870s.

4   Terz model body size with 11 1/2-inch width at lower bout and 22-inch scale. Listed from 1857 until the mid-1890s.

5   Terz model body size with 11 1/4-inch width at lower bout and 22-inch scale, e.g., 5-18. Listed from 1854 until 1990.

7   Baby dreadnought body size (about 7/8 of regular D-size) with 13 11/16-inch width at lower bout and a 23-inch scale, e.g., 7-28. First listed in 1980.

B   Jumbo-size body (see J) 4-string acoustic bass with 34-inch scale, e.g., B-65. First listed in 1989.

BC   Cutaway variant of B body, e.g., BC-40

C   Archtop guitar with 15-inch wide body and a 24.9-inch scale based on 000 flat-top, e.g., C-3. Available from 1931 until 1942 with either a round soundhole or a pair of f-holes.

After WWII, if placed before the body size, C indicates a cedar top rather than a spruce top, e.g., CHD-28. May also indicate a classical guitar, e.g., C-1R, CTSH.

After WWII, if placed after the body size, C indicates a cutaway body, e.g., OMC-28. A 2C-prefix indicates a double cutaway body, e.g., M2C-28.

CEO   Limited edition model designed by Martin's current chief executive officer, C.F. Martin IV, i.e., CEO-1 from 1997

CF   Newly designed archtop guitars introduced in 2004, e.g., CF-1 and CF-2

CHD   Dreadnought body with a cedar top, scalloped braces, and the old-style herringbone trim, e.g., CHD-35

CMJ   Custom jumbo-size body (see J) with, inter alia, a cherry sunburst finish, and white binding, e.g., CMJ-65

D   Dreadnought body size (initially spelled "Dreadnaught") with 15 5/8-inch width at lower bout and 25.4-inch scale, e.g., D-28. Introduced in 1916 on the Martin-made Ditson guitars. First listed in 1931 on Martin-branded instruments.

D12   Dreadnought body size with reinforced top bracing for 12-string variant, e.g., D12-20 first listed in 1964

DC   Dreadnought body with a cutaway, e.g., DC-28. First listed in 1981.

DCM   Cutaway Dreadnought body from the 1990s Road Series with laminated mahogany back and sides

DM   Dreadnought body from the 1990s Road Series with laminated mahogany back and sides

DR   Dreadnought body from the 1990s Road Series with laminated rosewood back and sides

DXM   Dreadnought variant from the X series with a body made of a wood fiber derivative material laminated under high-pressure

E   Used between 1979 and 1983 on the E-18 and E-28 solid-body electrics (also EM-18 with Mighty Might pickups)

EB   Used between 1979 and 1983 on the EB-18 and EB-28 solid-body electric basses

EMP   Model designed by a special task force of Martin employees, e.g., EMP-1. Introduced in 1998.

F   Archtop guitar with 16-inch wide body, 24.9-inch scale, and twin f-holes. Available from 1935 until 1942, e.g., F-9.

After WWII, the F-prefix refers to a thin-bodied electric with a 2-inch rim, available between 1961 and 1965, e.g., F-55

GT   Thin-bodied electric guitar with a 2-inch rim, available between 1965 and 1968, e.g., GT-75

HD   Dreadnought body with the old-style herringbone trim, maple bridge plate, and scalloped braces. First used on the HD-28; introduced in 1976.

HJ   Jumbo body with the old-style herringbone trim, e.g., HJ-28

HOM   OM body with the old-style herringbone trim, e.g., HOM-35

HP   Guitar with a herringbone pearl purfling, e.g., HPD-41

J   Jumbo body size with 16-inch width at lower bout and 25.4-inch scale, combining the shape of the M-series with the greater body depth of the Dreadnought. First listed in 1985 with an M- suffix, e.g., J-21M, later deleted by 1990.

J12   Jumbo body size with reinforced top bracing for 12-string version, e.g., J12-65

JC   Jumbo body with cutaway (see J), e.g., JC-40

L   Placed before the body size, an L-prefix used to refer to a top made of larch rather than spruce, e.g., LHD-28.

Since 2003, primarily applied to the "little Martin guitar" in the X series derived from a 0-14 fret tenor guitar and fitted with a 23-inch scale neck, e.g., LXM, LXK2.

M   Grand auditorium body size with 16-inch width at lower bout and 25.4-inch scale, similar in shape to the F archtops of the pre-war era, e.g., M-38. First listed in 1977.

MC   Grand Auditorium body with a cutaway, e.g., MC-28. The first Martin flat-top ever with a cutaway introduced in 1981

N   Classical guitar body size with 14 7/16-inch width at lower bout and 26.375 inch scale, e.g., N-20. First listed in 1968.

OM   Orchestra Model, i.e., 000 body with 14-fret neck and 25.4-inch scale. First listed as OM in 1930, e.g., OM-28.

R   Archtop guitar with 14 5/8-inch body based on 00 flat-top, available from 1933 until 1942 with a round soundhole or a pair of f-holes, e.g. R-18.

SOM   Used in 1977 to indicate the special order reissue of the OM-45 model briefly designated SOM-45

SP   Special variant of the 16 series guitars from the 1990s, e.g., SP000-16TR, SPD16TR, SP000C16TR

SW   Sustainable wood model, i.e., guitar made with woods like solid machiche, cherry, or katalox; e.g., SW00DB, SWDGT

STYLE NUMBERS IN MODEL DESIGNATIONS

1 D-1 original designation of D-18 proto in 1931
Archtop C-1 from 1931 to 1942
Archtop F-1 from 1940 to 1942
Contemporary 1 Series introduced in 1992
e.g., D-1, J-1, 000-1, B-1, C-1R

2 D-2 original designation of D-28 proto in 1931
Archtop C2 from 1931 to 1942
Archtop F-2 from 1940 to 1942
Contemporary 1 Series guitars with D-28 styling, e.g., D-2R

3 Archtop C3 from 1931 to 1934
Contemporary 1 Series guitars with D-35 styling, e.g., D-3R
Today, more generally indicates a guitar with a three-piece back as used on the D-35, e.g., DM3, M3H, M3M

7 Archtop F-7 from 1935 to 1942
Since 2005, refers to the 7-string Roger McGuinn models with a double G string tuned an octave higher, e.g., HD7

9 Archtop F-9 from 1935 to 1942

10 Classic N-10 from 1968 to 1993

15 First listed in 1935; phased out in 1963, e.g., 5-15, 0-15
Reintroduced in 1998, e.g., D-15

16 First listed in 1961, e.g., 0-16, 00-16, 000-16, D-16

17 First listed in 1856; phased out in 1897
Reintroduced in 1908; phased out in 1968, e.g., 5-17, 1-17, 2-17, 00-17
Special order 00-17 between 1982 and 1988

18 First listed in 1857, e.g., 5-18, 1-18, 0-18, 00-18, 000-18, D-18, J-18, OM-18

19 First listed in 1977; phased out in 1988, e.g., D-19 only

20 19th-century style listed in the 1850s, e.g., 2-20
Reintroduced in 1964 and phased out in 1991 on D12-20
Classic N-20 introduced in 1968

21 First listed in 1869, e.g., 1-21, 2-21, 00-21, 000-21, D-21, J-21

22 Listed in the 1850s

23 Listed in the 1850s

24 Listed from the 1850s to the 1880s, e.g., 2-24

25 First listed in 1980; phased out in 1989, e.g., 00-25K(2), D-25K(2)

26 Listed from the 1850s to the 1890s, e.g., 1-26

27 First listed in 1857; phased out in 1907, e.g., 1-27, 2-27

28 First listed in 1870, e.g., 5-28, 1-28, 0-28, 00-28, 000-28, D-28, OM-28, MC-28

30 First listed in 1870; phased out in 1921, e.g., 1-30, 2-30, 00-30, 000-30

33 19th-century style listed in the 1880s and 1890s

34 First listed in the 1860s; phased out in 1937, e.g., 5-34, 2-34, 1-34, 0-34, 00-34

35 First listed in 1965, e.g., D-35, M-35 (1978 only)

36 First listed in 1978; phased out in 1997, e.g., M-36 only

37 First listed in 1980; phased out in 1989, e.g., 7-37K, D-37K(2)

38 First listed in 1977, e.g., M-38 only

40 First listed in 1874; phased out in 1917
Reintroduced in 1928; phased out in 1941
Listed again in 1985
e.g., J-40, D-40, B-40

41 First listed in 1969, e.g., 00-41, 000-41, D-41

42 First listed in 1870; phased out in 1942, e.g., 00-42, 000-42
D-42V in 1985 and D-42LE in 1988

44 First listed in 1913; phased out in 1939, e.g., 0-44, 00-44

45 First listed in 1904; phased out in 1942
Listed again in 1968
e.g. 0-45, 00-45, 000-45, OM-45, D-45

50 Thin-body electric F-50 from 1961 to 1965. Used since 2001 for the superlative D-50 Deluxe edition guitars

55 Thin-body electric F-55 from 1961 to 1965

60 First listed in 1989; phased out in 1996, e.g., D-60 only

62 First listed in 1986; phased out in 1996, e.g., D-62 only

64 First listed in 1985; phased out in 1996, e.g., M-64 only

65 Thin-body electric F-65 from 1961 to 1965
Listed in 1985; phased out in 1996, e.g., J-65M, J12-65, B-65

68 First listed in 1985 on MC-68 only

70 Thin-body electric GT-70 in 1965–1966

75 Thin-body electric GT-75 in 1965–67

76 D-76 only as Bicentennial model in 1975–1976

93 D-93 only as Martin 160-year commemorative model in 1993

100 First used in 2004 on the superlative D-100 limited edition model derived from the 1,000,000th Martin guitar and numbered #1,000,001 to #1,000,050

111 Used in 2007 on the reissue of the 12-fret X-braced dreadnought originally made for the Oliver Ditson Company of New York

PRE-1898 GUITARS

Martin guitars made from 1833 until 1898 can be primarily identified by:

(i) the lack of serial number on the neck block;
(ii) their "New York" stamps and/or paper label;

which explains why they are often collectively referred to as New York Martins, even though most of them were actually built in Nazareth. They are fairly small guitars by modern standards, as 00 was the largest size available at the end of the 19th century. Finally, they were meant to be played exclusively with gut strings, as Martin did not switch to steel strings until the 1920s.

In any case, precisely assessing the date of issue of a pre-1898 instrument is quite difficult, unless it features a date penciled on the underside of the soundboard or an original sale receipt. Otherwise, for those who are not among the true Martin cognoscenti, determining the decade of issue is probably the best that can be achieved.

MAIN SUFFIXES IN MODEL DESIGNATIONS

A Body with non-standard ash back and sides, e.g., D-16A

AR Body made with Amazon rosewood instead of Brazilian or East Indian rosewood, e.g., D-42AR, OM-42AR

B Body with Brazilian rosewood back and sides as opposed to Indian rosewood; Brazilian rosewood was discontinued as standard after 1969, e.g., HD-35B.

BK Body with an overall black finish, e.g., J-40BK

BLE Limited Edition with Brazilian rosewood back and sides, e.g., HD-28BLE from 1990

BSE Signature Edition with Brazilian rosewood back and sides, e.g. HD-28BSE from 1987

C Used from the early 1960s to the early 1970s to indicate a classical variant meant for gut strings as opposed to steel strings, e.g., 00-28C

CTB Custom tortoise-bound body, e.g., HD-28CTB from 1992

D Used in the mid-1970s to indicate electrified variants of the D-18, D-28, and D-35

DB Deep body like a D or J model on a guitar usually built with a shallower body depth, e.g.,D-16DB

DLX Indicates special Deluxe appointments (such as extra pearl work) on some pre-war models, e.g., OM-45DLX

E Used between the late 1950s and early 1970s to indicate a flat-top model, factory-equipped with pickup(s), e.g., D-28E

Used again since the 1990s to indicate a guitar factory-built with onboard electronics, e.g., DC-1E

Also used occasionally to indicate a special model made for Martin employees, e.g., the Bicentennial D-76E from 1976

EST Body with top-grade Engelmann spruce top, e.g., HD-35EST

FM Body with figured maple, e.g., 00-16DBFM

FMG Body with figured mahogany back and sides, e.g., D-40FMG

FW Body with figured walnut back and sides, e.g., D-40FW

G Originally used from the mid-1930s to the early 1960s to indicate a guitar meant for gut strings as opposed to steel strings, e.g., 00-18G

GE Model with Golden Era 1930s-style appointments, i.e., a V-shaped neck, a forward-shifted X-bracing, scalloped braces, vintage-style tuners, etc., e.g., 000-28GE

GM Grand Marquis appointments, i.e., 45 style with herringbone top trim, rosette, and backstrip; tortoise binding; and pickguard; e.g., HD-28GM

GT Guitar with a gloss top finish when the model normally does not come with one, e.g., D-16GT

H Originally used to indicate a guitar with a Hawaiian setup (i.e., a high nut and saddle), e.g., 00-40H

Used more recently to indicate a guitar unusually fitted with herringbone backstrip and rosette, e.g., D-16H

K Originally used from 1917 to the 1940s to indicate a model entirely made of Hawaiian koa wood, e.g., 00-28K

Used since the 1980s to indicate a body with koa back and sides (but a spruce top), e.g., D-25K

K2 Used since the 1980s to indicate a body entirely made of koa wood (including the top), e.g., D-37K2

KLE Limited Edition with koa back and sides, e.g., D-45KLE

L Factory-made left-handed guitar with reverse nut, bridge, and top bracing, e.g., D-18L

LE Limited Edition, e.g., D-45LE from 1987

LSH Dreadnought body with, inter alia, a soundhole larger than the standard 4-inch diameter and herringbone top trim, e.g., D-28LSH from 1991

LSV Vintage series Dreadnought guitar with a soundhole larger than the standard 4-inch diameter, e.g., HD-28LSV from 1997

M Used in the 1980s to indicate the optional mahogany top on a model like the D-19. Also indicates a body unusually made of mahogany, e.g., HD-28M. Used in the 1990s to indicate a laminated mahogany body in the 1 series.

MB Indicates a guitar with maple binding on the body and a maple veneer on the peghead, e.g., D-18MB

MC Used from 1986 to 1990 on cutaway Jumbo models, e.g., J-21MC

N Used since the 1990s to indicate a regular neck as opposed to the (standard) low profile neck, e.g. D-45N

Also used in the designation of the HDN "negative" model made with a polished black lacquer body and polished ivory colored Micarta for the fingerboard, bridge, and pickguard.

May also signal a guitar made for nylon strings, e.g., 000C-16SGTNE

NY New York model characterized by a wide 12-fret neck with slotted headstock and no position markers, e.g., 0-16NY

P Originally used to indicate a 4-string plectrum model with a 27-inch scale, tuned C-G-B-D or D-G-B-D, e.g., 000-18P

Used since the mid-1980s to indicate a guitar fitted with the low-profile neck with a thinner radius introduced after Martin switched to an adjustable truss rod, e.g., HD-28P

PSE Signature Edition with a low-profile neck, e.g., HD-28PSE

Q Used since the mid-1980s to indicate a guitar fitted with the old-style non-adjustable neck reinforcement, e.g., D-18Q

Also used to signal a body made of quilted mahogany such as Graham Nash's signature 000-40Q2GN

QM Body with quilted maple back and sides, e.g., D-40QM

R Indicates on certain models a rosewood body, e.g., D-16TR

2R Body fitted with two rings of herringbone around the soundhole, e.g., HD-282R

S Originally used in pre-Custom Shop days to indicate a guitar built with special, non-standard appointments, e.g., D-45S from 1937 with a solid peghead. Mostly used since 1967 to indicate the early Dreadnought variant with a 12-fret neck, a wider nut width, a body with slope shoulders, and a slotted peghead, e.g., D-18S

SE Signature Edition, e.g., HD-28SE from 1986 autographed by C.F. Martin III and IV, and factory foremen

ST Model with Stauffer-style appointments such as the limited editions 00-45ST and 00-40ST issued in 1997

SW Special Wurlitzer models made in the 1960s for the E.U. Wurlitzer Company in Boston, e.g., D-28SW

T Originally used to indicate a 4-string tenor model with a shorter 22 1/2- to 23-inch scale, tuned C-G-D-A or later, D-G-B-E, e.g., 2-18T. Used since the 1990s to indicate the novel "Technology" neck joint of the 1-series, e.g., D-16T.

TSH Classical model built in cooperation with luthier Thomas Humphrey, e.g., C-TSH

V First used in 1983 to indicate vintage appointments such as a squared peghead, V-shaped neck, forward-shifted scalloped X-bracing, a long bridge saddle, aging toner lacquer on the soundboard, and vintage-style tuners, e.g., D-18V

VM Indicates a model with vintage-style appointments and a solid mahogany body, e.g., D-18VM

VMS Indicates a model with vintage-style appointments (ditto VM) on the S variant of the dreadnought body style, e.g., D-18VMS

VR Indicates a vintage reissue model with appointments such as a V-shaped neck, ivoroid binding, open tuning gears, a long bridge saddle, a shell-like pickguard, and aging toner lacquer on the soundboard, e.g., OM-28VR

VS Indicates a model with vintage-style appointments on the S variant of the Dreadnought body style, e.g., HD-28VS

W Body with walnut back and sides, e.g., D-16W

X Refers to the models from the X series made with a durable high-pressure wood fiber laminated body, e.g., DXM, LX1E, 000CXE

Date on Soundboard

A fair number of guitars built in the 1880s and 1890s feature a date penciled on the underside of the soundboard between the bridge and the soundhole (in either one of the outer sides of the X-bracing). This date is usually expressed with figures, e.g., 6/1888 or 7/91, and often appears with the initials of Frank Henry Martin (1866–1948). Penciled dates, sometimes fully completed to the day (e.g., 11/13/18) continued into the beginning of the 20th century, often with the initials of foremen (e.g., J.H.D. stands for John Deichman), but they ceased to appear after the 1920s.

New York Stamps and Labels

The early guitars from the 1830s (i.e., the only Martins actually made in New York) usually have a paper label glued inside the body. This label may come in various styles reflecting the various partnerships in which C.F. Martin, Sr. was then involved, but it always shows a New York address, i.e.:

- C. FREDERICK MARTIN or C.F. MARTIN at 196 Hudson Street
- MARTIN & BRUNO at 212 Fulton Street
- MARTIN & SCHATZ at 196 Hudson Street or no address
- MARTIN & COUPA at 385 Broadway

Some of the guitars from this period are also stamped with "C.F. MARTIN NEW YORK" on the outside of the back next to the neck heel.

Paper labels like Martin & Coupa survived into the 1840s and even into the very early 1850s. By 1852 paper labels were completely discontinued on 19th-century Martin instruments. The guitars without labels usually feature three semi-circular brand stamps reading "C.F. MARTIN NEW YORK" in the following places:

- on the center backstrip inside the body
- on the neck block
- on the back of the peghead

but the latter is sometimes replaced by a stamp on the outside of the back next to the heel, on the guitars with a birch or a maple neck stained black (as opposed to a cedar neck).

Although C.F. Martin moved from New York to Nazareth in 1839, all the guitars built through 1898 carry a "New York" stamp, presumably because of the distributorship agreement with a New York firm called C.A. Zoebisch & Sons.

- From the 1830s until 1867 the semi-circular stamps read "C.F. MARTIN NEW YORK"

- From 1867 until 1898, the stamps on the backstrip and on the neck block were changed to "C.F. MARTIN & Co. NEW YORK" when the elder Martin formed a partnership with his son and a nephew. But the stamps on the back of the peghead or on the outside back of the body remained unchanged.

- In 1898, when F.H. Martin ended the agreement with the New York-based Zoebisch, the stamp was changed again to "C.F. MARTIN & Co. NAZARETH, PA." in all places. The same year a serial number was first applied to all Martin guitars.

Headstock Shape and Style

The guitars from the 1830s and 1840s reflect the influence of Viennese luthier Johann Stauffer, for whom C.F. Martin worked before he emigrated to New York. One of their most striking features is an asymmetrical scrolled or S-shaped peghead with all the tuning keys on the bass side, albeit with a short treble E-string after the nut and a long bass E-string. In 1997 the Martin Company produced the limited edition 00-40ST and 00-45ST with Stauffer-style appointments to pay a tribute to the earliest designs of C.F. Martin, Sr.

A slotted headstock with three tuners on each side appeared in the 1840s and gradually became the norm during the 1850s when the scrolled peghead was completely phased out. C.F. Martin also began using squared-off solid pegheads with ivory friction tuners, albeit less frequently than the slotted headstock.

The scroll-shaped peghead of the 00-45 Stauffer issued in 1997 as a limited edition

Slotted headstock with "torch" pattern inlay

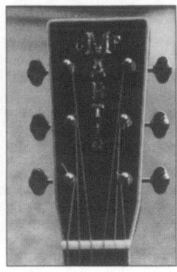

Headstock with the vertical C.F. Martin pearl logo originally introduced on the C-series archtops in 1931

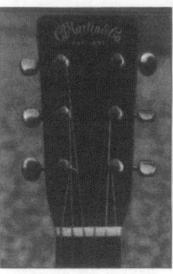

Solid peghead with the gold C.F. Martin & Co. decal introduced in 1932

Herringbone backstrip

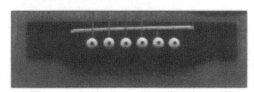

The thin "pyramid" bridge with pointed tips at each end.

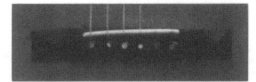

The (bottom) "belly" bridge introduced in 1929

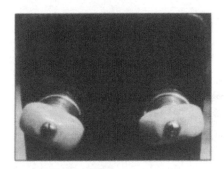

A modern rendition of the same design as found on the 1994 OM-40 Limited edition

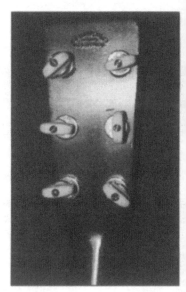

The rear headstock of a 1931 OM-18 with banjo tuners

Body Shape and Size

The Stauffer influence shows also in the body of the 1830s guitars that have a near-symmetrical shape, almost like a figure 8, with similar upper and lower bouts of about 11 to 12 inches wide. The back and sides of the earliest guitars are often made of maple. Later instruments have a rosewood back and sides with an inner spruce lamination inside the body. The upper bout was narrowed on 1840s instruments to break away from early European influences, and by the early 1850s sizes were first standardized.

From the mid-1850s until the 1880s, sizes 2 and 2½, respectively with a 12-inch and 11 5/8-inch width across the lower bout, were the most popular sales-wise. Size 0 and size 1, respectively with a 13.50-inch and a 12.75-inch body width, took over in the 1880s and 1890s as demand for larger guitars gathered pace among musicians. The larger 00 size with a 14 1/8-inch bottom bout was first listed in the early 1870s, but very few examples from the 19th century exist, and presumably very few were made.

For the record, the hallowed herringbone ornament of German origin was first used in the late 1860s as a regular appointment on the rosette and backstrip of styles 20-21-22-23, and on the top binding of styles 28 and 30. Before the late 1860s, herringbone trim may be found on the body back, while half-herringbone patterns were also used on the top and on the rosette.

Neck and Fretboard

All the Martin guitars from the 19th century feature a 12-fret neck of classical inspiration. The earliest necks are made of maple, birch, or any other whitish wood, and are often stained black. They are sometimes adjustable via an amazing clock-key (hence the screw neck designation), which remained as an option into the 1890s although it became quite scarce after the 1830s, presumably because of cost.

The earliest models often display a typical angle-cut ebony fretboard with a 21- or 22-fret extension touching the soundhole. Later instruments from the 1830s, with a Stauffer headstock but a regular fingerboard, were at first built with 20 frets, but the last guitars with a scrolled peghead usually feature 18 frets.

The paper label found on the 1994 OM-40LE

The two-piece cedar neck with grafted headstock, and its typical long dart or diamond volute, only appeared in the late 1840s on the better models. When body shapes and styles were standardized in the early 1850s, sizes 1, 2, and 3 were all fitted with 18-fret ebony fretboards. Only the larger size 0, first listed in 1854, and size 00, first listed in 1873, were built with a 19-fret fingerboard during the 19th century. The traditional 20-fret fingerboard only appeared at the beginning of the 20th century on Martin guitars.

Besides the number of frets, another typical characteristic of the 19th century Martins is the absence of inlays on the fingerboard until the late 1890s. And even then, in a typically restrained manner, only the top-end style 42 was adorned with three pearl inlays at the 5th, 7th, and 9th frets.

Bridge Design

The earliest Stauffer-influenced bridge is narrow and thin with ornamental pointed ends. The strings are held in place by ebony pins with pearl inlays. Before the end of the 1830s this design was superseded by a slightly wider bridge with rounded ends and a pointed bottom center. This second variant is usually made of ebony, but it can also be found in ivory with pearl-inlaid ivory bridge pins.

The brown paper label of the highly successful 000-42EC from 1995, Martin's first signature model

The rounded bridge design continued into the 1840s, a period during which Martin first introduced a narrow rectangular bridge with a Spanish-style flat anchoring of the strings as opposed to vertical pins. This newer design, made of ebony or ivory, was actually the first version of the famous pyramid bridge that would remain Martin's staple design, albeit with pins, from the late 1840s until the inception of the belly bridge in 1929. The "pyramid" nickname originates in the small ornamental pyramid tip sculpted at each end of the bridge.

Top Bracing

Early Martins from the 1830s usually have a ladder bracing with the braces perpendicular to the strings. Some rare early models are built with a classical-type fan strutting, inspired by the Spanish school. During the 1840s C.F. Martin, Sr. gradually developed his famous X-bracing that can be found on some mid-1850s instruments. Fan braces, however, remained standard on all the lower-end models such as style 17, 18, and even 20. Only the upper-end styles with a larger body were consistently fitted with the novel X-brace design.

1830s guitar in the Stauffer style. Note the scroll-shaped peghead, the extended fingerboard, the near symmetrical body shape with a narrow waist, and the long bridge with thin pointed ends.

1915 00-42 with ivory bridge and ivory friction tuners

OM-45 made circa 1930, one of the first Martin guitars with a 14-fret neck

Modern D-28 with herringbone trim around the top edge of the body (HD-28)

1918 5-21

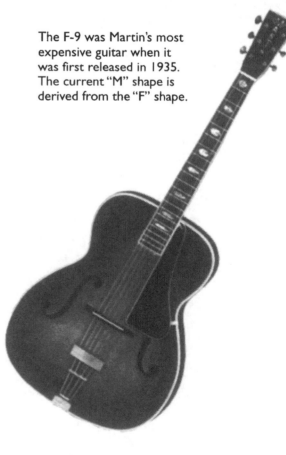

The F-9 was Martin's most expensive guitar when it was first released in 1935. The current "M" shape is derived from the "F" shape.

1919 0-30 with slotted headstock and pyramid bridge

Original 12-fret D-45 made in 1937. Out of the 91 D-45s made before WWII, only three of them were released with a 12-fret neck and extended body.

A fairly rare variant of the high-end D-45 with a shaded top

1967 GT-75 double cutaway electric with DeArmond pickups and bolt-on neck

00-45 style guitar custom-made with walnut back and sides and a highly unusual brown finish on the top. The underside of the top is penciled with "J.A.P. 11/13/1918."

000-45 made in 1934, featuring the vertical C.F. Martin pearl inlay

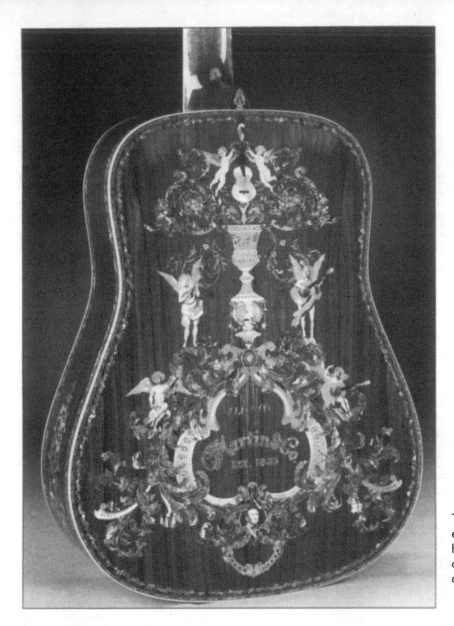

The milestone millionth Martin guitar is the most elaborate instrument ever made in the company's history. This spectacular Dreadnought was unveiled on January 15, 2004, and took nearly two years to complete.

ABOUT THE AUTHOR

André Duchossoir is the author of several guitar books: *Gibson Electrics: The Classic Years*, *The Fender Stratocaster*, and *The Fender Telecaster*. He has also contributed to other guitar books like *Gibson Guitars: 100 Years of an American Icon* by Walter Carter, *Classic Guitars of the '50s* and *Classic Guitars of the '60s* edited by Tony Bacon, and *Echo and Twang—Classic Guitar Music of the '50s*, also edited by Tony Bacon.

SUGGESTED READING

The following books are recommended as further reading to obtain detailed information on the various models made by Fender, Gibson, Gretsch, and Martin.

Fender

Bacon, Tony. *50 Years of Fender: A Half Century of the Greatest Electric Guitars*. San Francisco: Backbeat, 2000.

————. *The Fender Electric Guitar Book*. Milwaukee: Backbeat, 2007.

————. *Six Decades of the Fender Telecaster: The Story of the First Solidbody Electric Guitar*. San Francisco: Backbeat, 2005.

Black, Jay W., and Albert Molinaro. *The Fender Bass: An Illustrated History*. Milwaukee: Hal Leonard, 2001.

Blasquiz, Klaus. *The Fender Bass*. Milwaukee: Hal Leonard, 1991.

Duchossoir, A. R. *The Fender Stratocaster*. Milwaukee: Hal Leonard, 1995.

————. *The Fender Telecaster*. Milwaukee: Hal Leonard, 1991.

Roberts, Jim. *How the Fender Bass Changed the World*. San Francisco: Backbeat, 2001.

Smith, Richard R. *Fender: The Sound Heard 'Round the World*. Milwaukee: Hal Leonard, 2003.

Wheeler, Tom. *The Stratocaster Chronicles: Celebrating Fifty Years of the Fender Strat*. Milwaukee: Hal Leonard, 2004.

Gibson

Bacon, Paul. *50 Years of the Gibson Les Paul*. San Francisco: Backbeat, 2002.

Carter, Walter. *The Gibson Electric Guitar Book*. San Francisco: Backbeat, 2007.

Duchossoir, A. R. *Gibson Electrics: The Classic Years*. Milwaukee: Hal Leonard, 1998.

Ingram, Adrian. *The Gibson L5: Its History and Its Players*. Fullerton, CA: Centerstream, 1997.

————. *The Gibson 175: Its History and Its Players*. Fullerton, CA: Centerstream, 2007.

————. *The Gibson 335: Its History and Its Players*. Fullerton, CA: Centerstream, 2006.

Iwanade, Yasuhiko. *The Beauty of the 'Burst*. Milwaukee: Hal Leonard, 1999.

Lawrence, Robb. *The Early Years of the Les Paul Legacy, 1915–1963*. Milwaukee: Hal Leonard, 2008.

————. *The Modern Era of the Les Paul Legacy, 1968–2007*. Milwaukee: Hal Leonard, 2009.

Scott, Jay, and Vic DaPra. *The Gibson 'Burst, 1958–1960*. Fullerton, CA: Centerstream, 2007.

Gretsch

Bacon, Tony. *50 Years of Gretsch Electrics*. San Francisco: Backbeat, 2005.

Scott, Jay. *The Guitars of the Fred Gretsch Company*. Fullerton, CA: Centerstream, 1992.

Martin

Carter, Walter. *The Martin Book*. San Francisco: Backbeat, 2006.

Longworth, Mike. *Martin Guitars: A History*. Revised and updated by Richard Johnston and Dick Boak. Milwaukee: Hal Leonard, 2008.

————. *Martin Guitars: A Technical Reference*. Revised and updated by Richard Johnston and Dick Boak. Milwaukee: Hal Leonard, 2008.

Washburn, Jim, and Richard Johnston. *Martin Guitars: An Illustrated Celebration of America's Premier Guitar Maker*. New York: Penguin, 2003

General

Bacon, Tony. *The Ultimate Guitar Book*. New York: Alfred A. Knopf, 1997.

Gruhn, George, and Walter Carter. *Gruhn's Guide to Vintage Guitars*. San Francisco: Backbeat, 1999.

Wheeler, Tom. *American Guitars: An Illustrated History*. New York: Harper Resource, 1992.

The Fender Bass
AN ILLUSTRATED HISTORY
by J.W. Black and Albert Molinaro
Hal Leonard
Using hundreds of photographs, this exciting release chronicles the evolution of that instrument from 1951 to 2001, providing background, history and highly researched facts vital to understanding everything about this remarkable member of the Fender family.
00330755 .... $24.95
(978-0-634-02640-9)

The Fender Electric Guitar Book – 3rd Edition
A COMPLETE HISTORY OF FENDER INSTRUMENTS
by Tony Bacon
Backbeat Books
This new edition marks Fender's 60th anniversary. It tells the story of the Telecaster, Stratocaster, Jazzmaster & other models via dozens of new photos and updated text.
00331752 .... $24.95
(978-0-87930-897-1)

The Fender Stratocaster
by A.R. Duchossoir
foreword by Eric Clapton
Hal Leonard
This best-seller features everything about this American classic: its history, patents and schematics, pricing, and handy identification tips. Includes stunning new full-color photos.
00330027 .... $15.95
(978-0-7935-4735-7)

50 Years of Fender
HALF A CENTURY OF THE GREATEST ELECTRIC GUITARS
by Tony Bacon
Backbeat Books
Featuring 200 color photos, this visual chronicle of the premier guitar maker charts every Fender model from 1950 to 2000, accompanied by a parallel timeline of musical highlights.
00330592 .... $22.95
(978-0-87930-621-2)

How the Fender Bass Changed the World
by Jim Roberts
foreword by Marcus Miller
Backbeat Books
Focusing on the bass' artistic influence, this book details the technical milestones that gave the bass its musical power. Loaded with black & white and 100 stunning color photos.
00330737 .... $27.95
(978-0-87930-630-4)

Six Decades of the Fender® Telecaster
THE STORY OF THE WORLD'S FIRST SOLIDBODY ELECTRIC GUITAR
by Tony Bacon
Backbeat Books
Packed with photos, collectable catalogs, period press ads, and memorabilia, this tribute tells the story of the Telecaster and the Fender Company through exclusive interviews with Fender figures who were there when this musical star was born.
00331298 .... $22.95
(978-0-87930-856-8)

The Soul of Tone
CELEBRATING 60 YEARS OF FENDER AMPS
by Tom Wheeler
Foreword by Keith Richards
Book/2-CD Pack
Hal Leonard
An authorized and illustrated book on the most famous amplifiers ever. Revered as much as one's guitar, the Fender amplifier gets its due in this full-color, richly illustrated book. Includes two CDs with over 120 tracks demonstrating terms and topics. Over 400 photos.
00331054 .... $60.00
(978-0-634-05613-0)

The Stratocaster Chronicles
CELEBRATING 50 YEARS OF THE FENDER STRAT
by Tom Wheeler
Foreword by Eric Clapton
Book/CD Pack
Hal Leonard
This authorized book/CD package offers the best photos, quotes, facts and sounds to celebrate the Strat's Golden Anniversary. Includes exclusive photos from the world's greatest guitar collection, as well as a CD with musical examples of famous Strat sounds and styles hilariously performed by Greg Koch.
00331056 .... $50.00
(978-0-634-05678-9)

The Fender Telecaster
by A.R. Duchossoir
Hal Leonard
The "Telly" is the senior member of a family of instruments that revolutionized popular music, and this book relates their story since 1950.
00183003 .... $15.95
(978-0-7935-0860-0)

GIBSON

50 Years of the Gibson Les Paul
HALF A CENTURY OF THE GREATEST ELECTRIC GUITARS
by Tony Bacon
Backbeat Books
The Gibson Les Paul turned 50 years old in 2002, and since its invention, its sweet, urgent sound has been used by a host of ma or rock players. Unique color photographs feature a multitude of luscious Les Paul models and highlight great players in action with their Les Paul guitars.
00330951 .... $22.95
(978-0-87930-711-0)

The Gibson Electric Guitar Book
SEVENTY YEARS OF CLASSIC GUITARS
by Walter Carter
Backbeat Books
The ibson Electric uitar Book is a comprehensive, richly illustrated guide to Gibson electrics past and present. Starting with the S-150 through the 5s, Les Pauls, SGs, Firebirds, and more, it is packed with facts, stories, and images that tell the story of Gibson's great guitars and their most famous and influential players.
00331792 .... $24.95
(978-0-87930-895-7)

Gibson Electrics
THE CLASSIC YEARS
by A.R. Duchossoir
Hal Leonard
This book presents a documented account of the instruments released during a highly creative period from the 19 0s up to the mid-60s. It describes all the models that have made history and contributed to establishing the reputation of Gibson.
00330392 .... $24.95
(978-0-7935-9210-4)

Gibson Guitars
TED MCCARTY'S GOLDEN ERA: 1948-1966
by il Hembree
foreword by eymour Duncan
H Books
As C O of Gibson from 194 to 1966, Ted cCarty presided over the production of nearly one million guitars and amps, considered to be some of the most valuable fretted instruments in the world. This is McCarty's first & only complete bio, featuring 100 photos from his personal archives.
00331465 .... $29.95
(978-1-4234-1813-9)

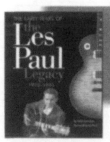

The Early Years of the Les Paul Legacy
1915-1963
by Robb Lawrence
Introduction by Les Paul
Hal Leonard
A beautiful book on the legendary inventor and musician and his partnership with Gibson to make the world's most cherished electric guitar. Features gorgeous original photographs, and insights and recollections from Les Paul, Michael Bloomfield, Jeff Beck, and others.
00330972 .... $40.00
(978-0-634-04861-6)

The Beauty of the 'Burst
by asuhiko wanade
Hal Leonard
This book is a tribute to Gibson's magnificent Sunburst Les Pauls made between 195 and 1960. Featuring lavish full-color photos, the guitars of famous players, a foreword by Ted c-Carty, and much more.
00330265 .... $34.95
(978-0-7935-7374-5)

GRETSCH

50 Years of Gretsch Electrics
by Tony Bacon
Backbeat Books
This fully-illustrated history book boasts great pictures of rare instruments, absorbing stories from the early days as well as Gretsch's latest exploits, and a collector's reference guide to every single instrument from the last 50 years.
00331258 .... $24.95
(978-0-87930-822-3)

Gretsch
THE GUITARS OF THE FRED GRETSCH CO.
by Jay cott
Centerstream Publications
This comprehensive, manual uncovers the history of the guitars through 2 pages of color photos, hundreds of black & white photos, and forewords by Fred Gretsch, George arrison, andy achman, rian Setzer, and Duane ddy.
00000142 .... $35.00
(978-0-931759-50-5)

MARTIN

The Martin Book
by Walter Carter
Backbeat Books
A fresh view of this extraordinary guitar maker, pulling together many strands of musical and manufacturing lore into a fascinating whole that illuminates artin's long and varied history.
00331417 .... $24.95
(978-0-87930-887-2)

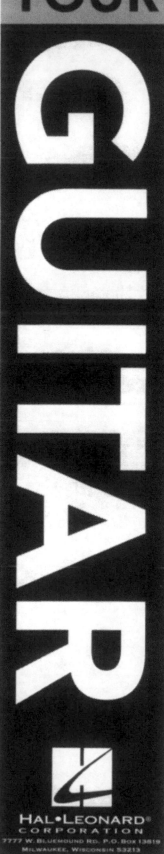